Mel Bay Presents Chet Atkins plays Back Home Hymns

Superb Guitar Renderings of Familiar Hymns

Note for note transcriptions in notation and tablature with performance notes

Transcribed by Jerry R. Ozee

1 2 3 4 5 6 7 8 9 0

© 2001 BY MEL BAY PUBLICATIONS, INC., PACIFIC, MO 63069.
ALL RIGHTS RESERVED. INTERNATIONAL COPYRIGHT SECURED. B.M.I. MADE AND PRINTED IN U.S.A.
No part of this publication may be reproduced in whole or in part, or stored in a retrieval system, or transmitted in any form
or by any means, electronic, mechanical, photocopy, recording, or otherwise, without written permission of the publisher.

Visit us on the Web at www.melbay.com — E-mail us at email@melbay.com

Table of Contents

Understanding the Tablature 3

Preface 4

Acknowledgements 5

Take My Hand Precious Lord 6

Amazing Grace 9

Will The Circle Be Unbroken 12

In The Garden 17

When They Ring The Golden Bells 21

Just As I Am 24

Further Along 26

Just A Closer Walk With Thee 31

The Old Rugged Cross 35

Lonesome Valley 38

God Be With You 43

Were You There 47

A Note From Craig Dobbins 50

A Note From Richard Hood 51

My Favorite Chet Album 52

About the Author 53

Discography 54

Liner Notes from the Original LP 55

Understanding the Tablature

Sometimes it is difficult to put into print all that the artist does to achieve the feeling and tone that make a recording a masterpiece. You will note in some of the selections that we have placed below the TAB lines either a "B" with a vertical arrow in the tab, or an "R" with a curved vertical line in the tab.

The "B" indicates the notes are "brushed" either with a sweep of the thumbpick or played with a combination of thumbpick and fingers sounding almost together but with a very slight separation of the notes.

The "R" indicates that a more distinct separation of the notes is achieved with the right hand (usually leading from bass to treble strings) but not as to produce a true arpeggio.

Whether one chooses to use the pick alone or combination of pick and fingers to achieve the effect is a matter of individual preference. Listen to the recording carefully, then use your own intuition to get the sound and feeling that works best for you. These symbols are placed into the tablature only as a reminder to avoid a "mechanical" technique when performing certain phrases.

As to left hand fingerings, especially for phrases of single notes, you may find it more desirable to play some notes in a different position. Individual preference is again the rule (the guitar as an instrument offers lots of options). Remember, when choosing a playing position, that the higher up the neck a note is produced the "fatter" and sweeter it sounds.

Preface

As the journey of life is lived, if one is exceptionally blessed, a real hero emerges who dramatically affects the thoughts and direction of that life. Chet Atkins has been that hero for me. From the first moment I heard him play in 1960, Chet has blessed my life. Such beautiful music played on the guitar calms and soothes the soul, endears the hero, enthrones the artist in the heart. And then when privilege and opportunity permit a personal relationship, the man himself transcends the artist. Fortunately this has been my journey.

Celebrity Star Status rightfully belongs to Chet, but his music takes all who know and love him beyond the surface glitter of fame to the recognition of his musical genius. And perhaps in none of his recordings do celebrity and musical genius emerge as much as when *Chet Atkins Plays Back Home Hymns*. The emotional sweetness, the spiritual intent of the composers and the purity of tone are masterfully produced.

Without elaborating on all of the tunes, suffice it to say that *Take My Hand Precious Lord* and *Were You There*, in a spiritual sense, take us all on a journey with Christ Himself. When you listen to this album, you are made to actually feel the presence of the Lord. The heart is made to overflow with the true sense of God's love. Only Chet can create such musical euphoria.

Now comes a gifted dentist from Illinois, Dr. Jerry Ozee, who has transcribed all these hymn classics to tablature for the guitar exactly as Chet recorded them. He has produced a masterful mentoring tool of musical enjoyment for all who love to play the guitar. Every guitarist who plays his way through the pages of this new book will be able to play the same notes and chords that Chet played. No, he probably won't have the same sound as the master, but he will have the chance to play, at his own level, Chet Atkins' wonderfully distinctive music.

Dr. Ozee is my friend and a talented guitarist who possesses unusual musical expertise. He not only loves Chet Atkins, the man, but also has a true appreciation for his artistry. His book is genuinely a labor of love that honors and perpetuates Chet's music. And it stands on its own as a marvelous musical achievement.

It is an honor and esteemed privilege to write the Preface on behalf of all those who think of Chet Atkins as their musical hero. Thank you, Jerry, and thank you, Mel Bay Publishing Company for this new publication. This book allows all of us to participate in a personal way in perpetuating the musical legacy of Chet Atkins as we all join our hero in playing Back Home Hymns.

And I say, as would Chet, "That's my opinion and it oughta be yours, too, don'tcha know!"

Bill Spann

Bill Spann is Master of Ceremonies for the annual Chet Atkins Appreciation Society Convention, which meets each summer in Nashville, Tennessee.

Acknowledgements

Dear Friends,

This book of hymn arrangements, as recorded by Chet Atkins, was done in hopes that other guitarists will benefit from the availability of beautiful hymns for guitar, both for use in worship services and for personal enjoyment as well. The arrangements have not been simplified, and are intended for use by those who know and appreciate Chet's style of guitar technique. I have transcribed these twelve selections exactly as Chet played them on the album *Chet Atkins Plays Back Home Hymns* (RCA LPM/LSP-2601), and carefully added fingerings and performance notes.

I would like to give special thanks to Chet and Leona Atkins for granting permission to put this work into written form so that everyone can enjoy learning and performing these superb hymn arrangements.

I also wish to thank everyone who helped in the preparation of this book, especially:

My wife, Shirley, for her patience with me as I labored alone over the transcriptions and manuscript;

My dear friends, Bill Spann, Master of Ceremonies for the Chet Atkins Appreciation Society Conventions, for his kind opening remarks for this work, and Richard Hood, for his enthusiastic support and comments;

My daughter Gretchen Cawthon, who so expertly set up the format of the book with her computer skills;

Don and Edna Comp, who have spent many hours searching for great photo opportunities of Chet and others, and who have generously offered many of their terrific photographs;

Gwen Peiper, who first inspired me to offer this work for publication, and who introduced me to the late Mel Bay and his son William Bay. Gwen also offered advice with the musical notation;

Jim Ferron and Dr. Mark Pritcher, founders of the Chet Atkins Appreciation Society, an organization which now hosts the world's biggest and best celebration of the guitar, and which has served as a vehicle for exchange of information and friendships for guitarists everywhere. The knowledge and friendships I have acquired at the annual conventions have certainly facilitated the birth of this book;

Craig Dobbins, creator and publisher of Acoustic Guitar Workshop, P.O. Box 8075, Gadsden, AL 35902, an experienced author, who shared with me essential advice about getting things into print;

The fine folk at Mel Bay Publishing Co., especially William Bay, Stephen Rekas, and Ed Riegler, who took on this idea with great enthusiasm, and meticulously guided me though the many steps of getting everything in order;

My many friends who enthusiastically offered support and encouragement;

And most of all, thanks to Chet Atkins for all the great music!

Jerry R. Ozee

Take My Hand Precious Lord

T. Dorsey
Arr. Chet Atkins

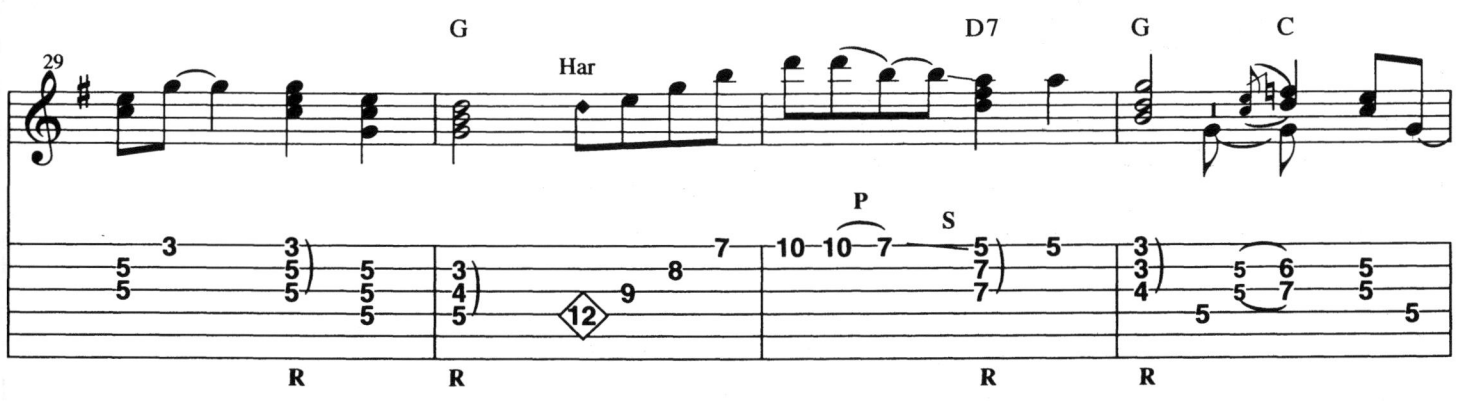

Performance Notes

At measure 30, Chet slips in a natural harmonic on the 4th string and finishes the arpeggio with pure notes. However, for effect, one can play the entire last half of measure 30 and the first half of measure 31 with natural harmonics by touching the various strings at the 7th and 12th frets with the left hand and sounding the notes with the right hand.

Amazing Grace

John Newton
Arr. Chet Atkins

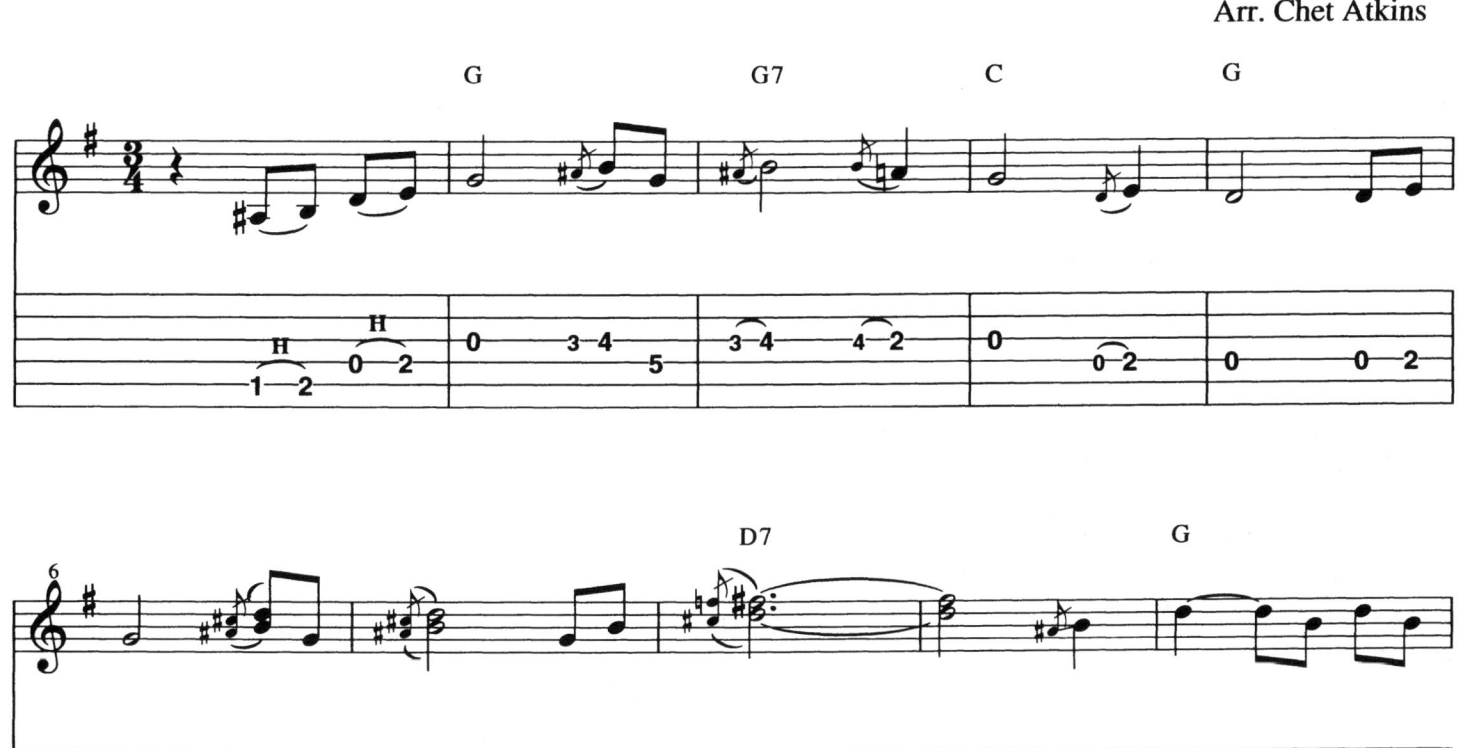

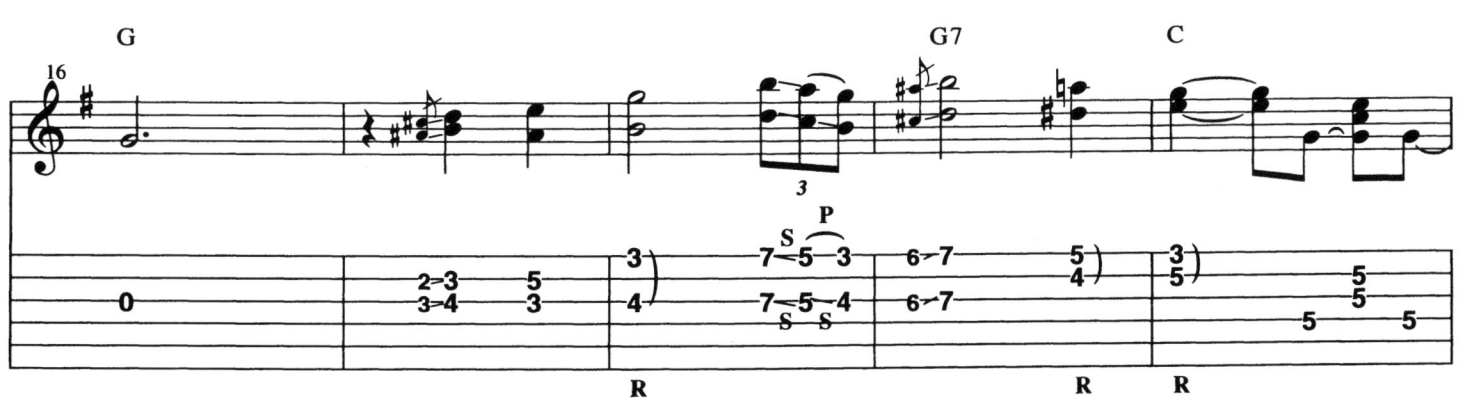

Arr. © 2001 by Athens Music Company. All Rights Reserved. Used by Permission.

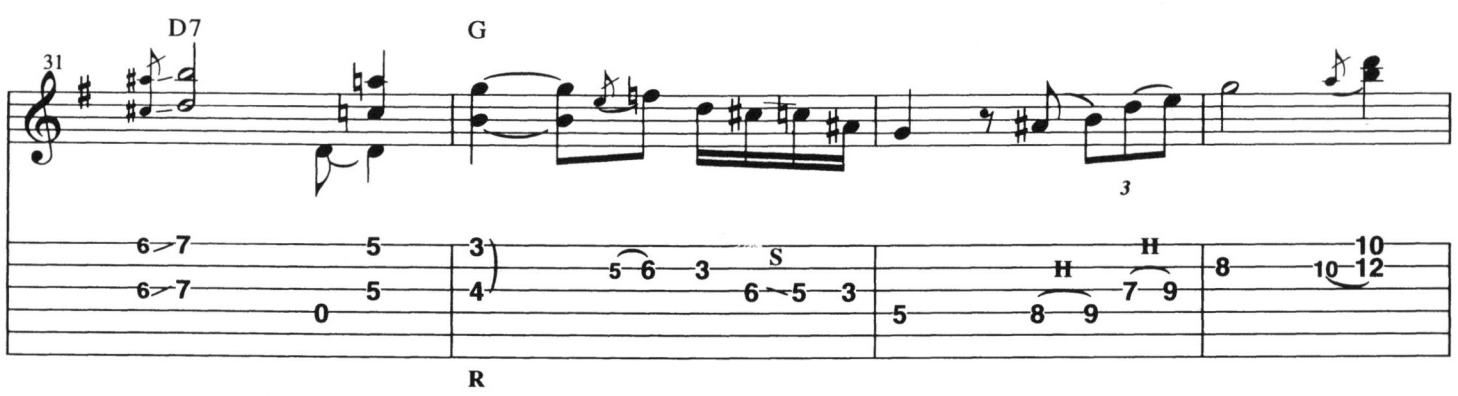
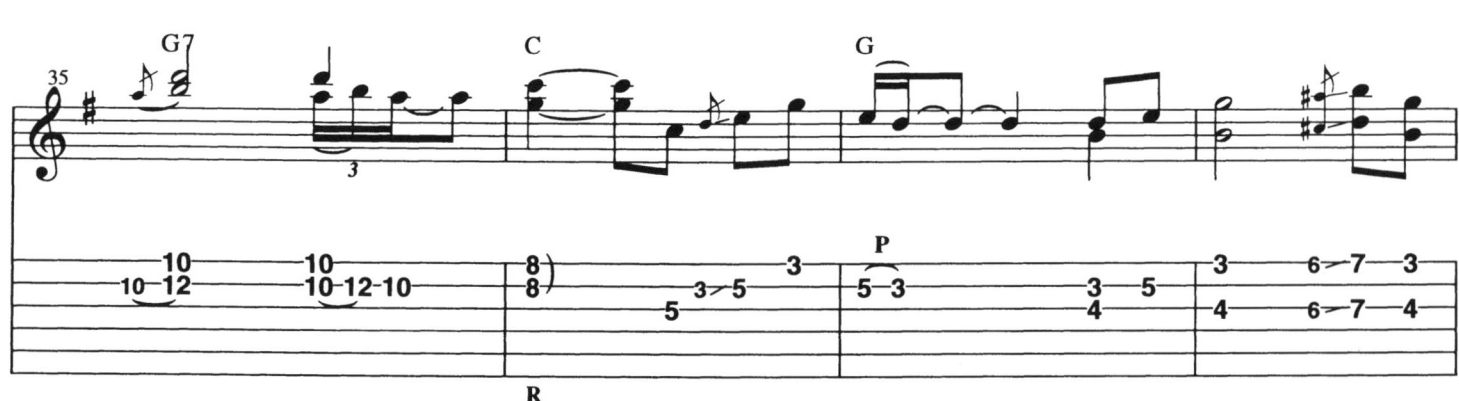

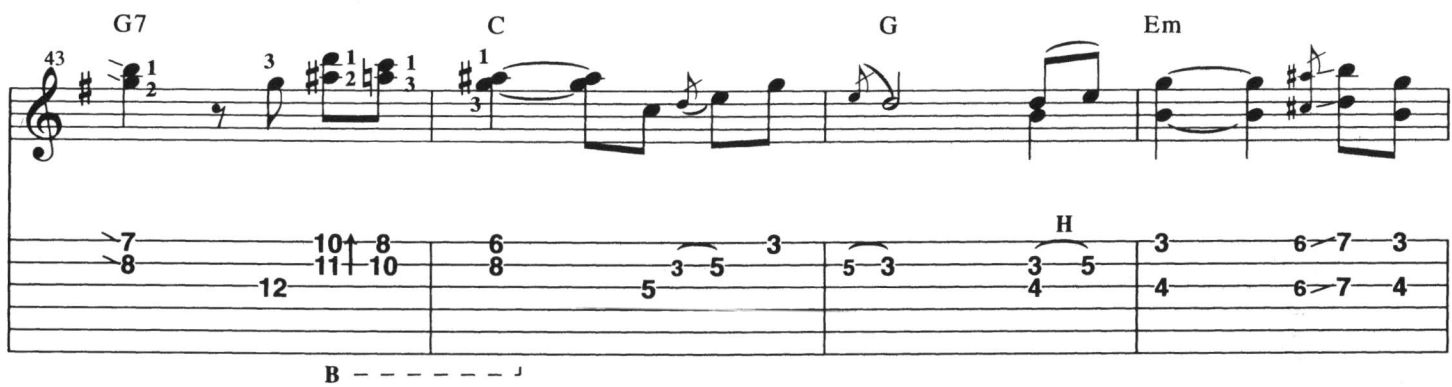
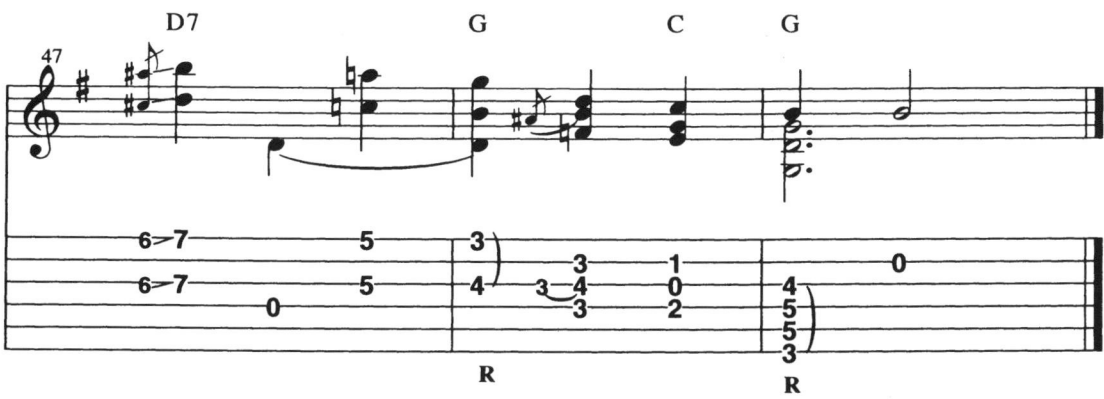

Performance Notes

The measures that account for the harmonica solo in the recording have been omitted from this transcription beginning at measure 33. Correct application of the left hand fingering measures 41-44 will be helpful. The suggested fingering is shown in the music staff.

Will The Circle Be Unbroken

Traditional
Arr. Chet Atkins

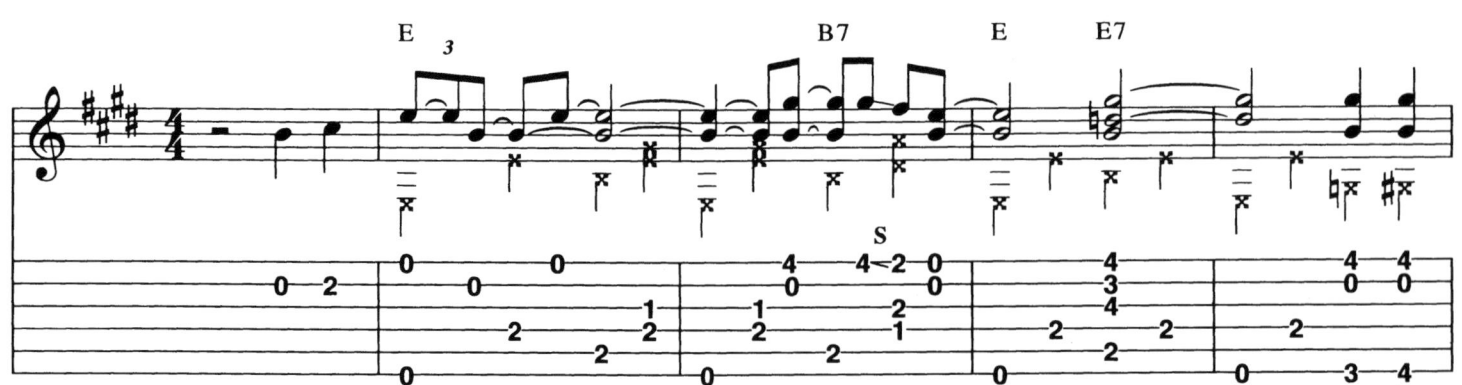

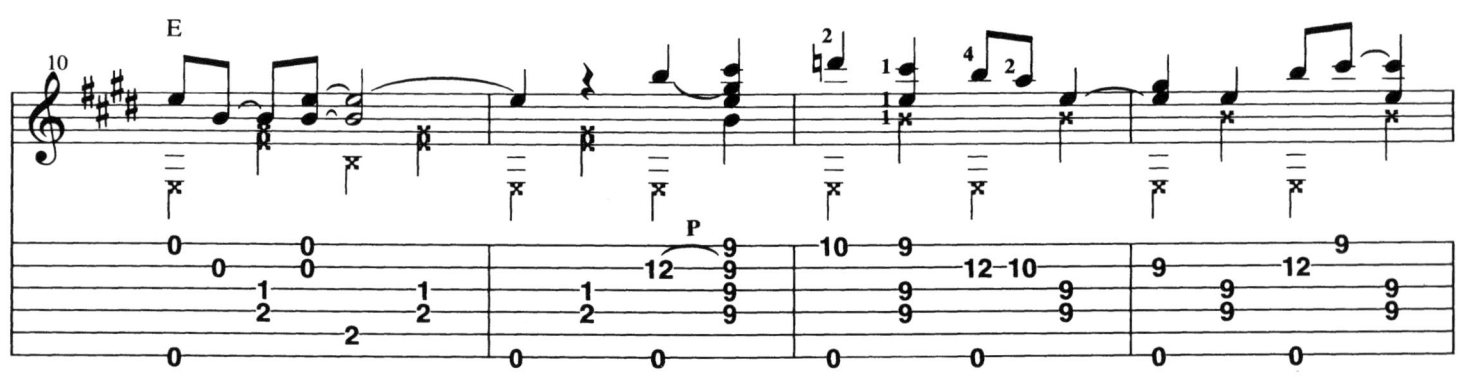
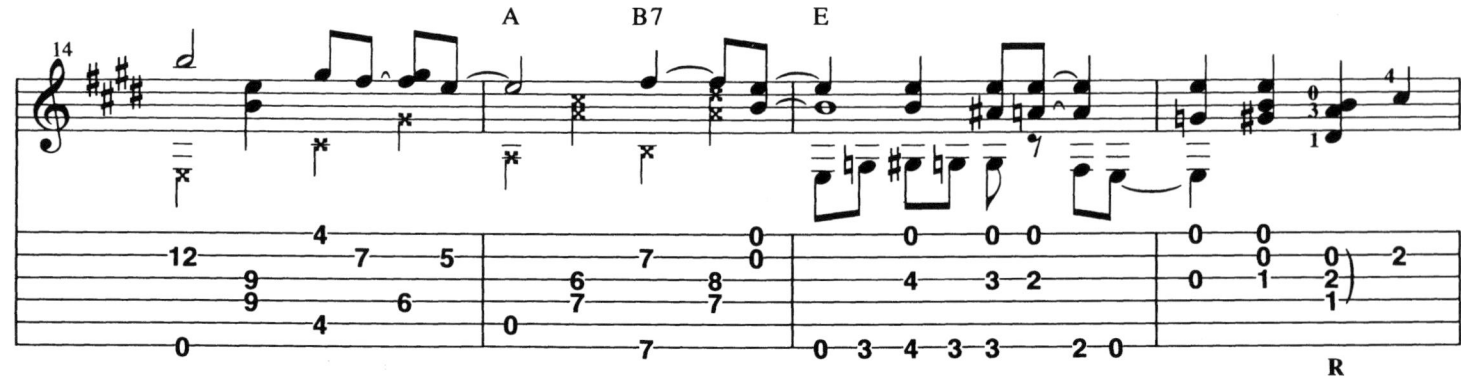

Arr. © 2001 by Athens Music Company. All Rights Reserved. Used by Permission.

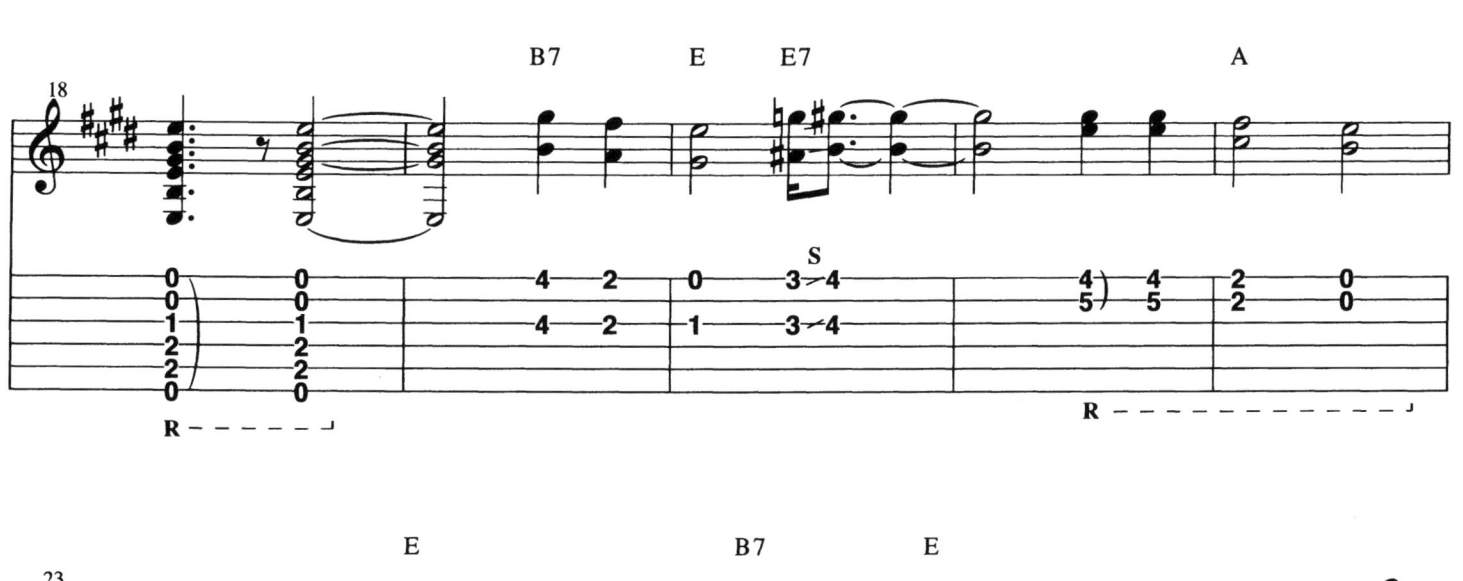
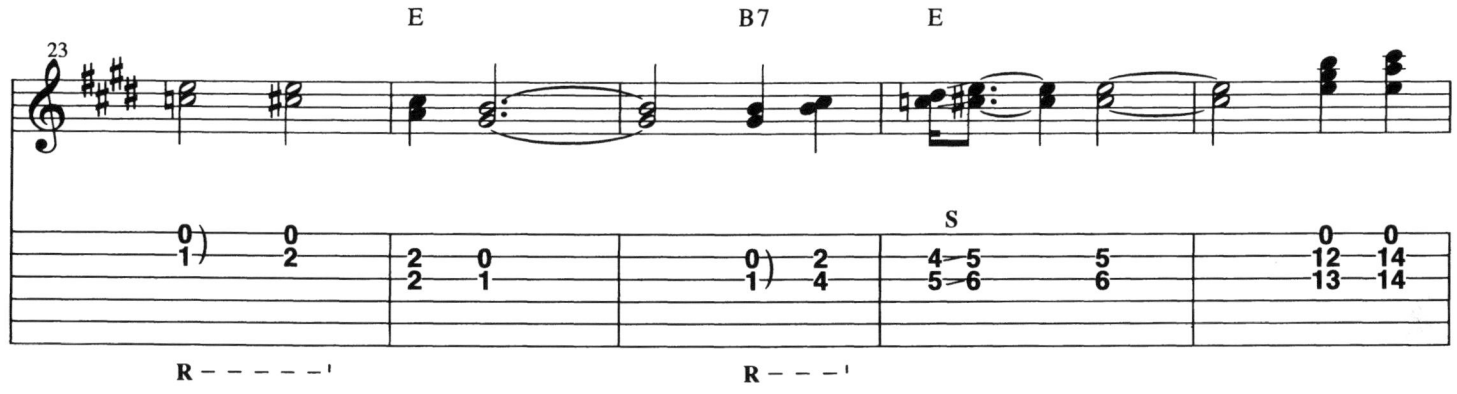
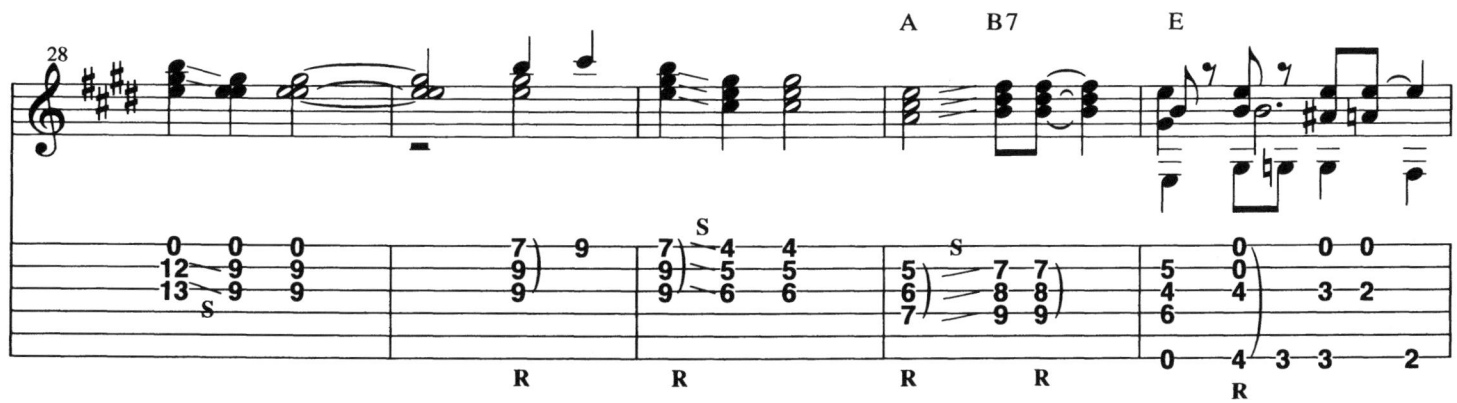

13

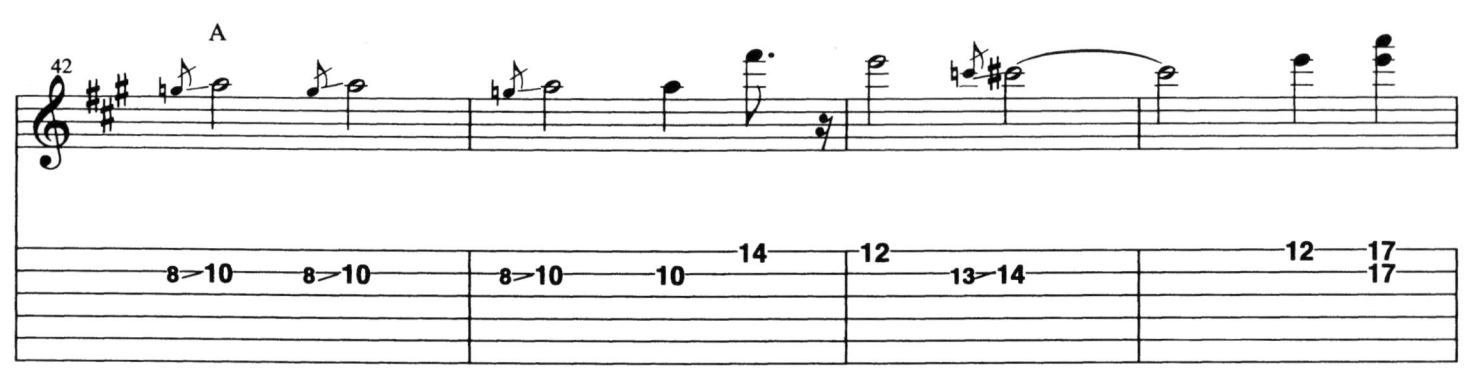
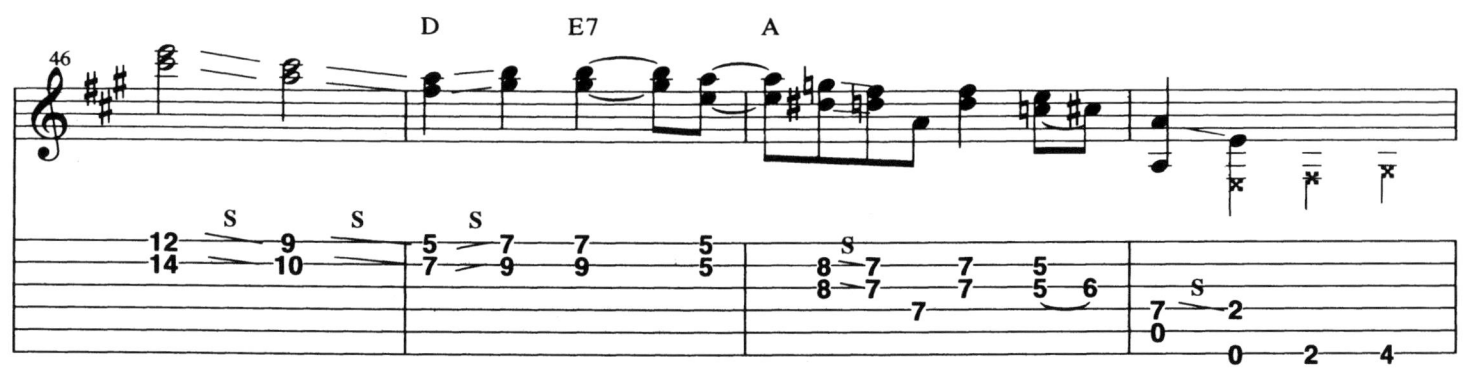
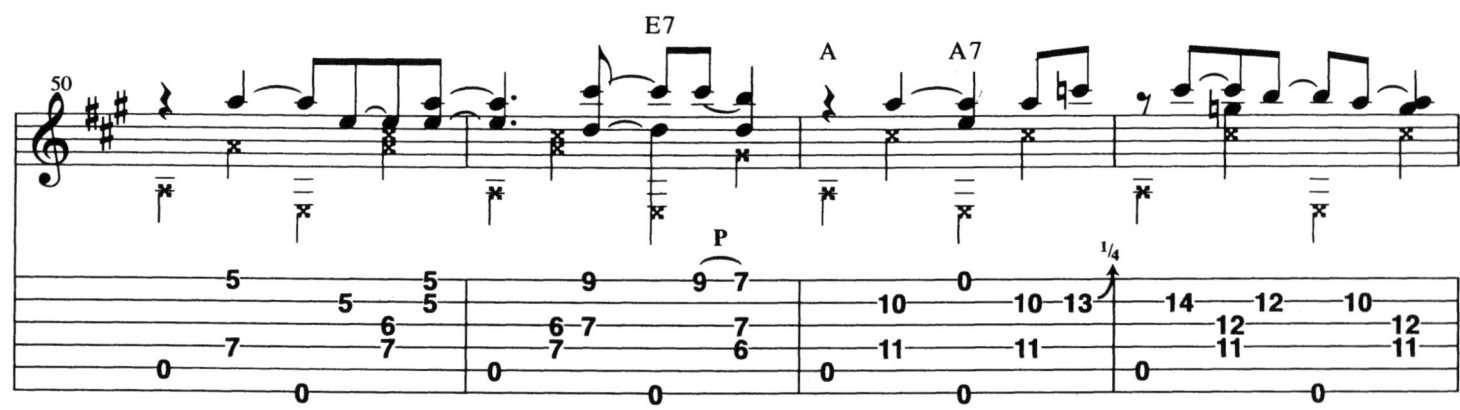

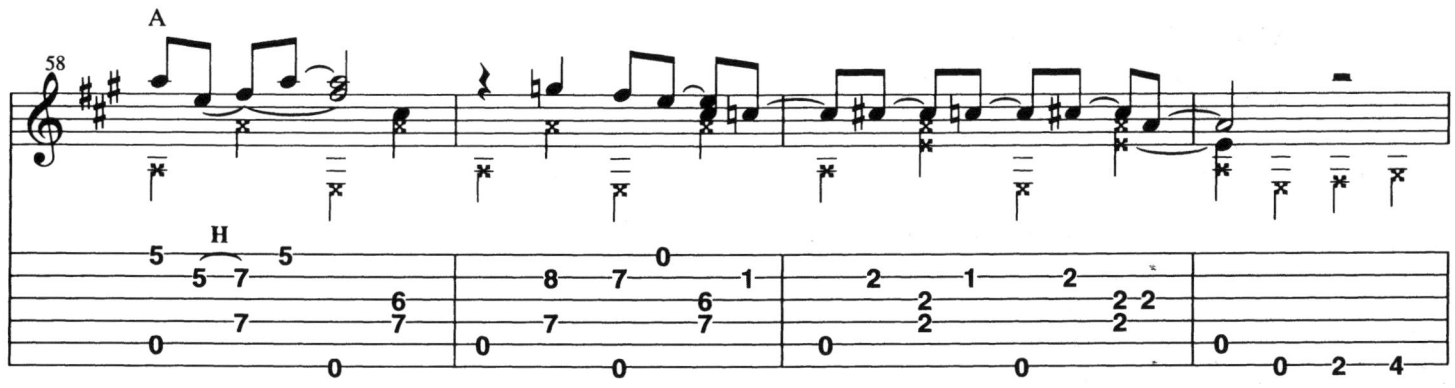
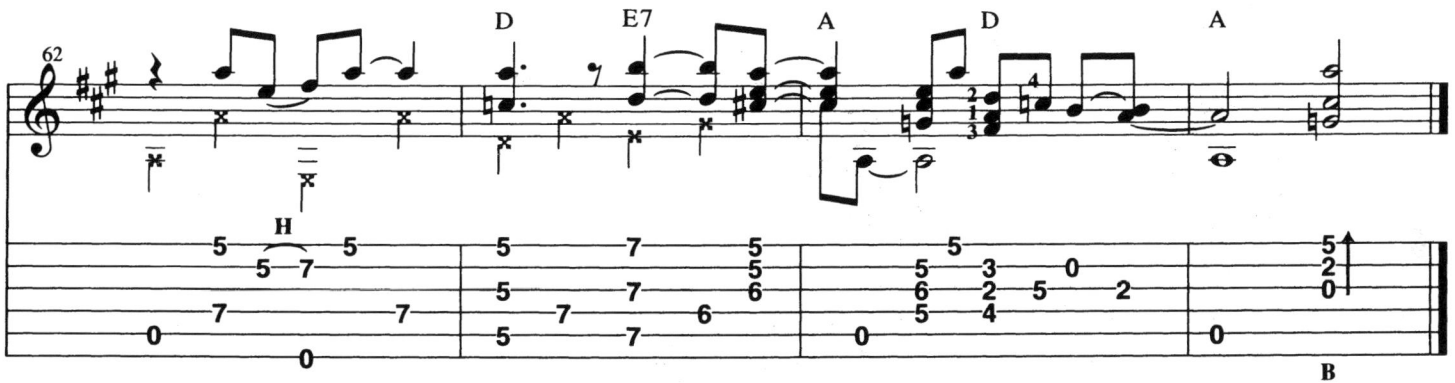

Performance Notes

This arrangement utilizes Chet's distinctive style of a steady rhythm alternating bass, which in 4/4 time is heard as "boom-chic, boom-chic." Be sure to muffle the bass strings with the palm of the right hand. The melody line is played with the fingers against the steady bass rhythm. To avoid a mechanical feeling to the performance, listen to the recording carefully and note how Chet "anticipates the melody" to achieve a more easy going feel. Part of the secret is that the melody notes seldom fall directly on a beat. This may mean that the right hand fingers often sound the strings just ahead of the thumb. After a little practice, the feeling should become spontaneous. These same techniques are used in the arrangement of "Lonesome Valley." The piece modulates to the key of A at measure 34 where in this transcription, the measures accounting for the harmonica solo in the recording have been deleted.

Touch of the Master's Hand

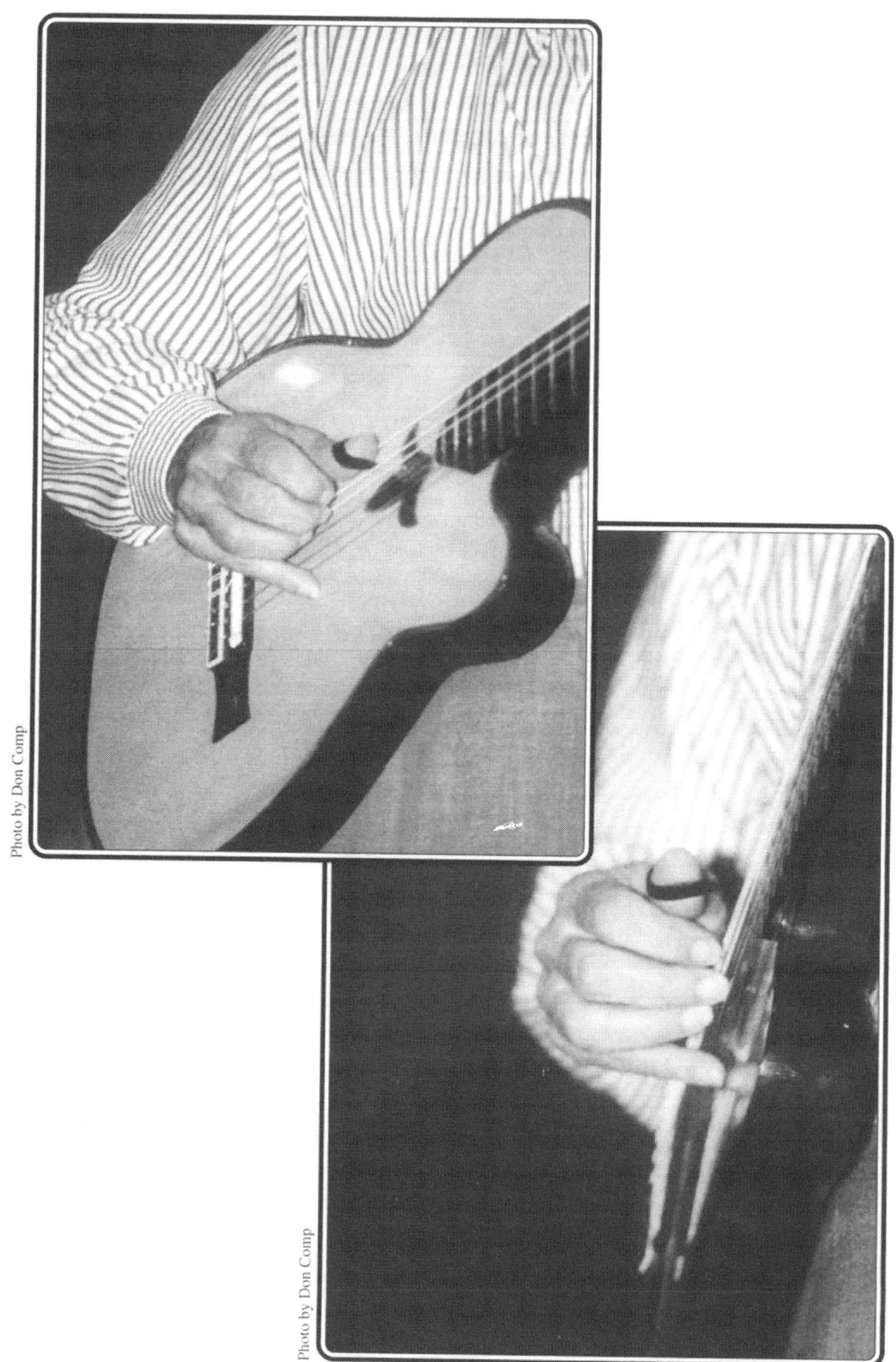

In The Garden

C. Austin Miles
Arr. Chet Atkins

Arr. © 2001 by Athens Music Company. All Rights Reserved. Used by Permission.

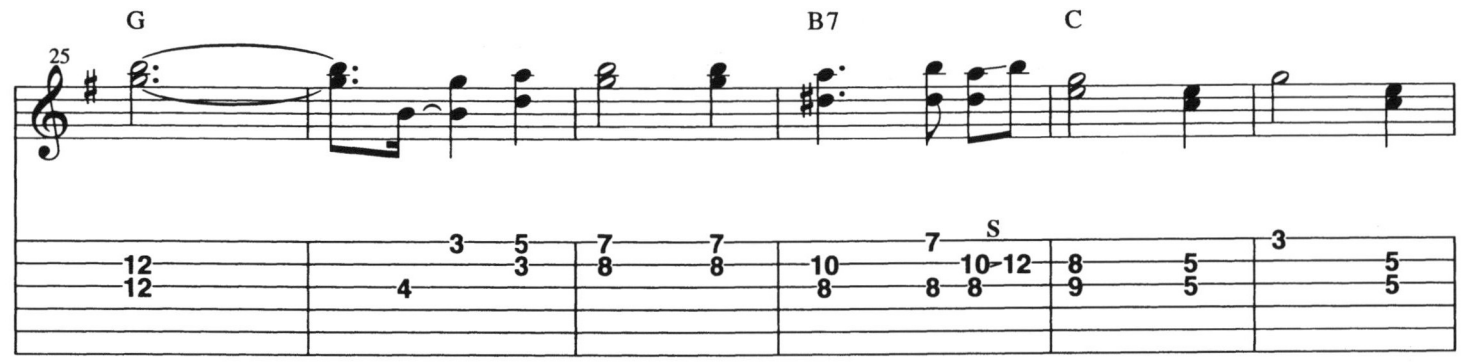
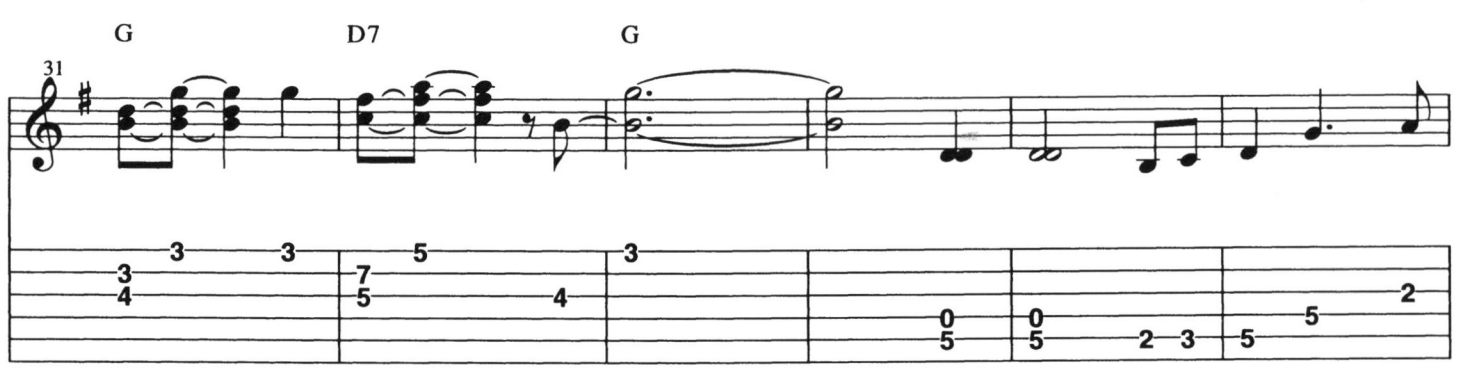
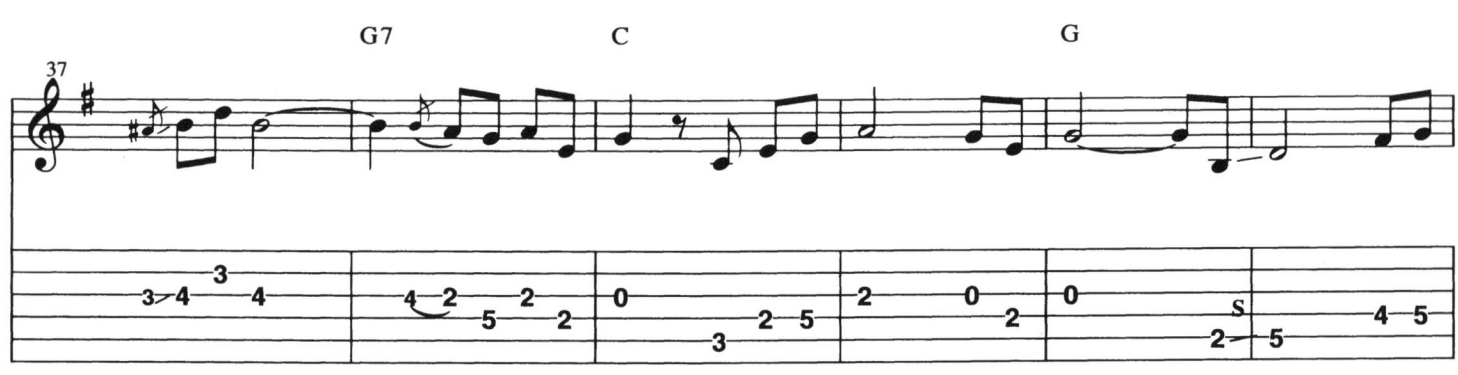
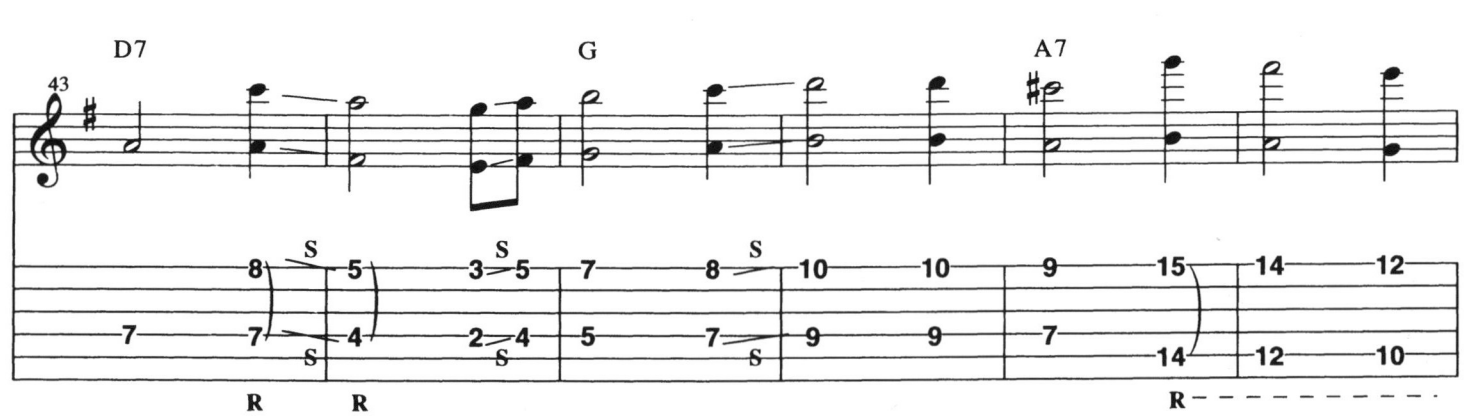

When They Ring The Golden Bells

Dion DeMarbelle
Arr. Chet Atkins

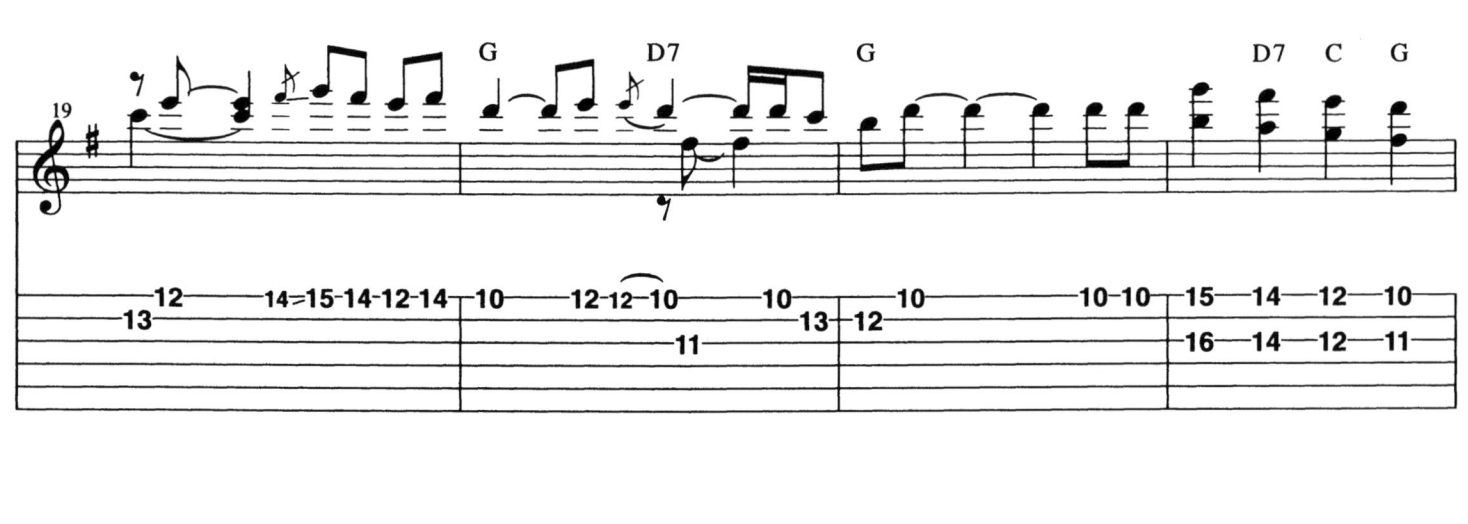
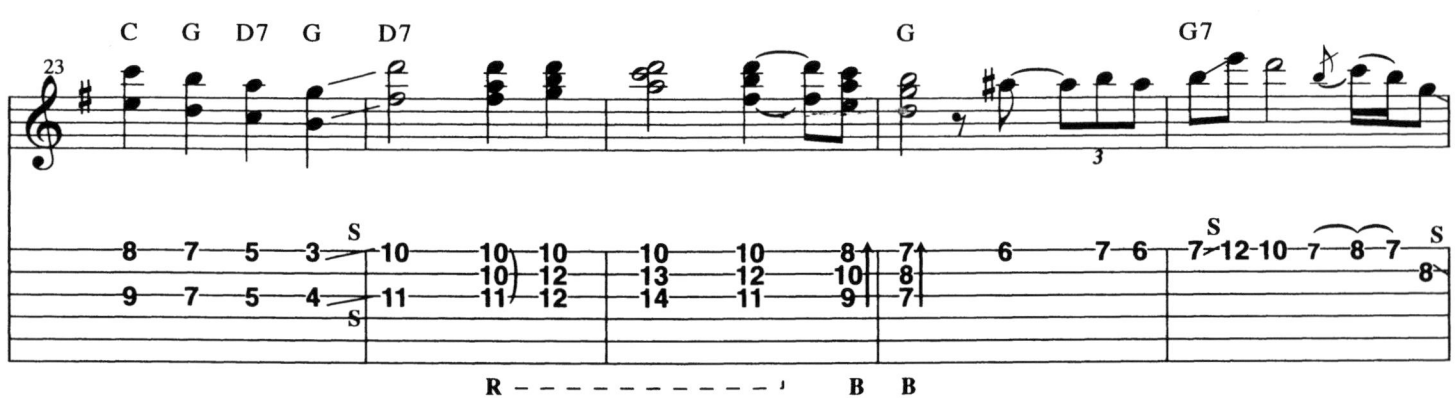
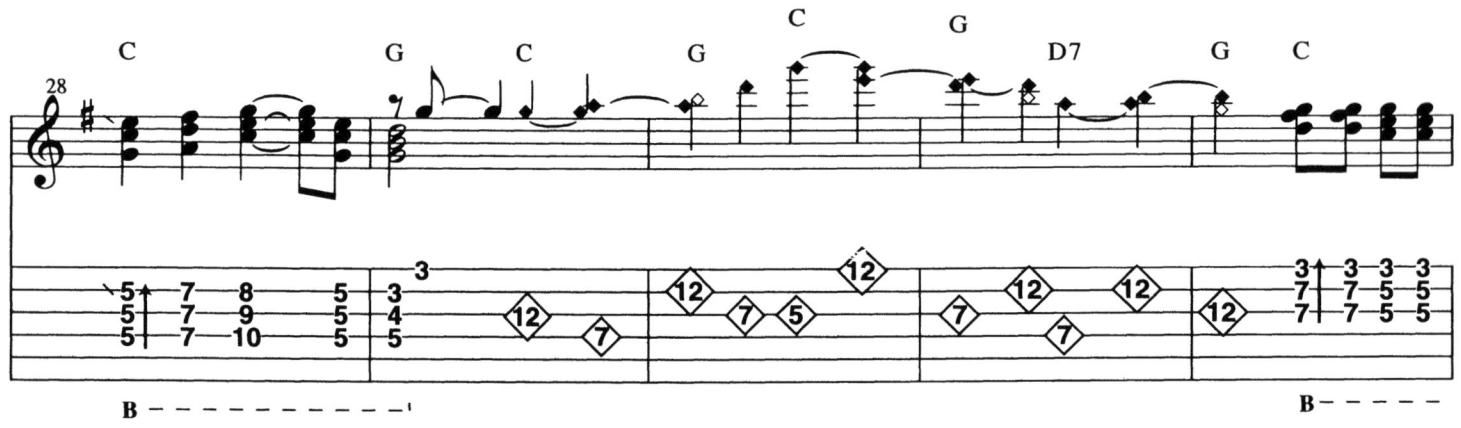

Notes with stems up in tab are Chet's harmonics

Bass notes (stems down) simulate piano in the recording

Performance Notes

Pay particular attention to the left hand fingerings shown by the numbers in the notation to achieve good tone and efficient left hand positioning. Your left hand will get a good stretch in measure 32.

Chet cleverly "rings the golden bells" with all natural harmonics in measures 29-32 and 45-50. The left hand touches a string at the twelfth (or seventh or fifth) fret while the right hand sounds the string.

In the recording, the piano carries the melody in measures 33 through 49, and the piano melody is here illustrated by the notes with stems down and is not intended to be played by the guitar.

Chet plays some beautiful "golden bells" accompaniment to compliment the piano and this is illustrated in these same measures by the notes with stems up. The technique requires one to play artificial harmonic notes and natural notes (or pure tones as Chet calls them) at the same time. To play an artificial harmonic, touch the string 12 frets above the tab number which is diamond shaped with the tip of your right index finger and play the note with your thumbpick while simultaneously plucking the natural notes with your right hand middle or ring finger, whichever you prefer. This same technique is also utilized in the selection *Just As I Am*, from the same album.

Just As I Am

C. Elliot & W. Bradbury
Arr. Chet Atkins

Arr. © 2001 by Athens Music Company. All Rights Reserved. Used by Permission.

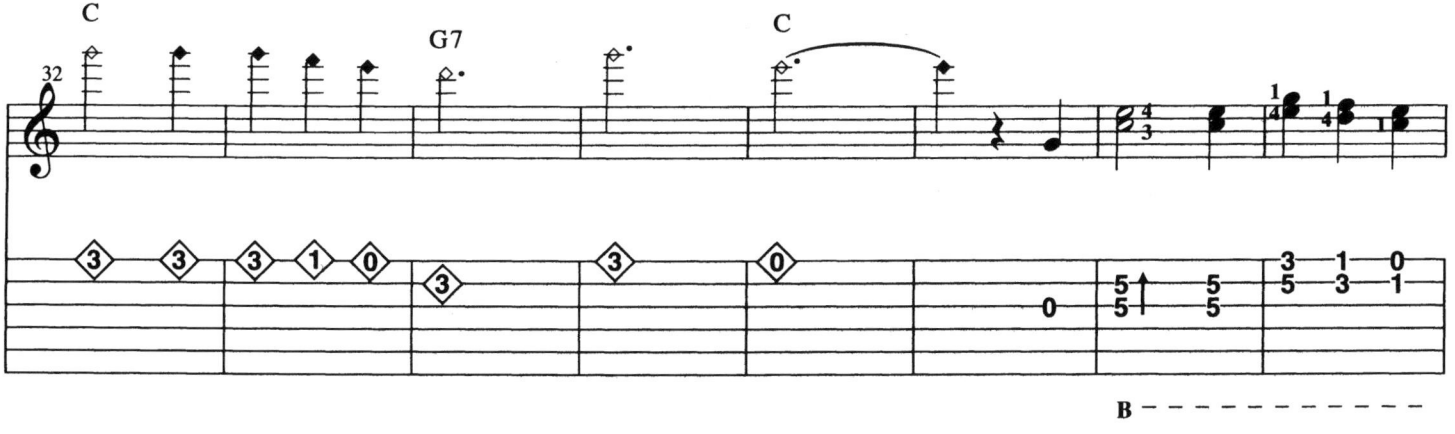
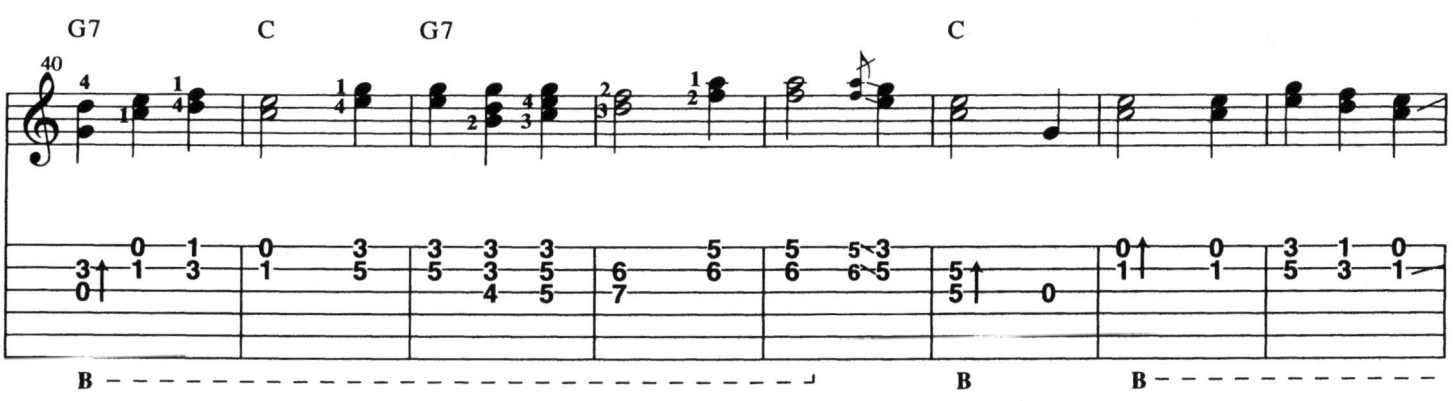

Performance Notes

This tune is played on electric guitar with tremolo. Beginning at measure 19 and continuing through measure 36, Chet carries the melody on the guitar with artificial harmonic notes. The harmony notes heard in the recording in this section were probably played on the Hammond organ or a vibraphone. To play an artificial harmonic, touch the string lightly 12 frets above the diamond shaped tab number with the tip of your right index finger, and play the note with your thumbpick. As the note is sounded, lift your right hand finger from the string and a bell-like tone will result.

Further Along

J.R. Baxter, Jr. and W.B. Stevens
Arr. Chet Atkins

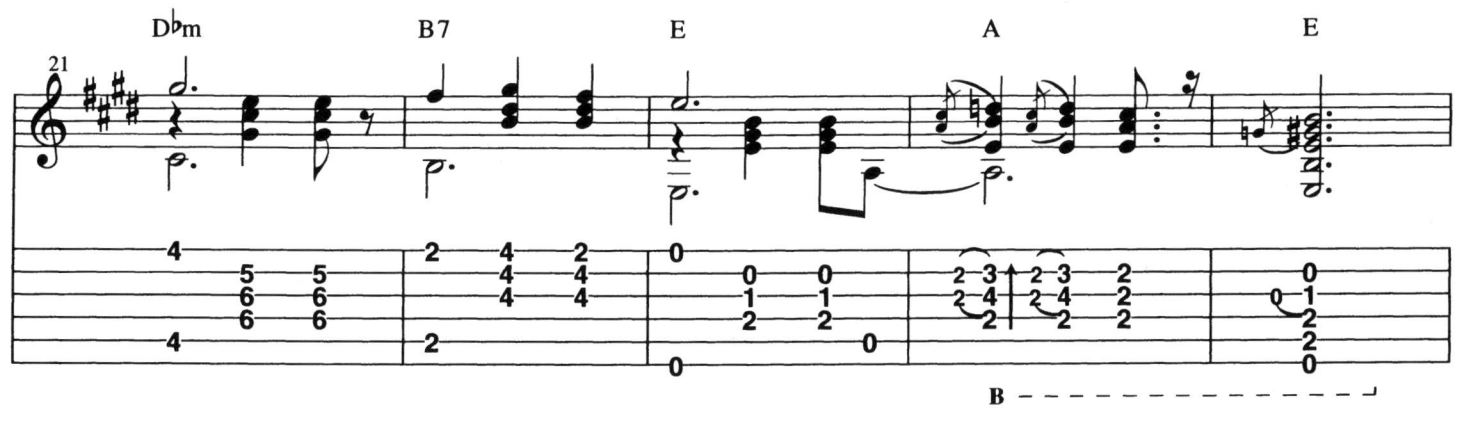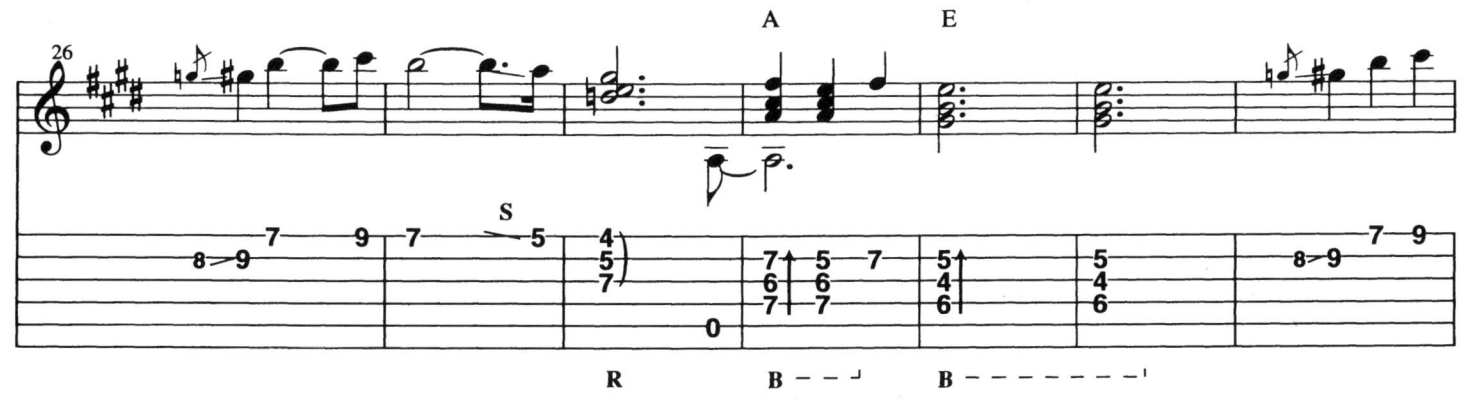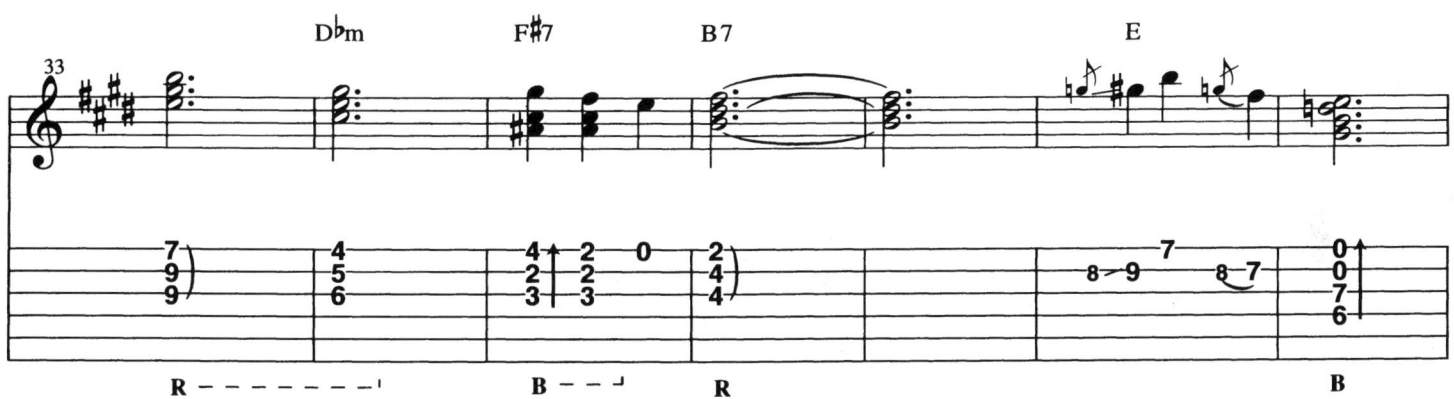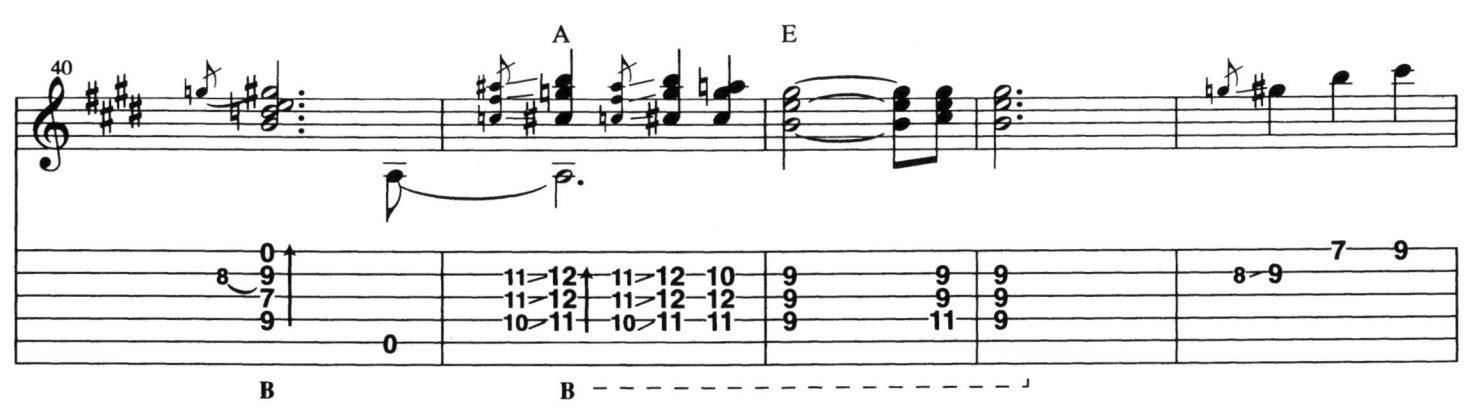

Harmonica solo arranged for guitar measures 50-73

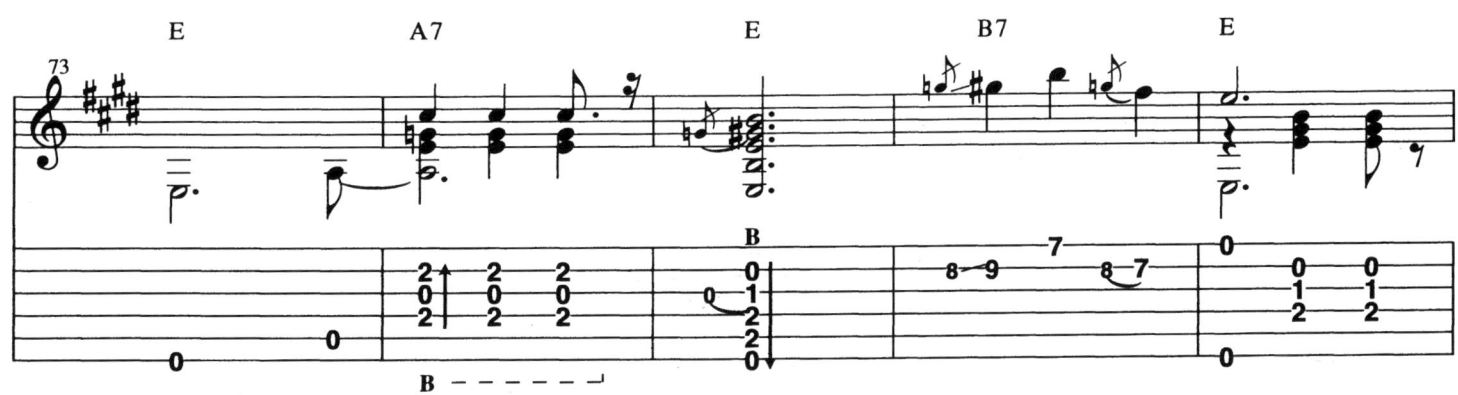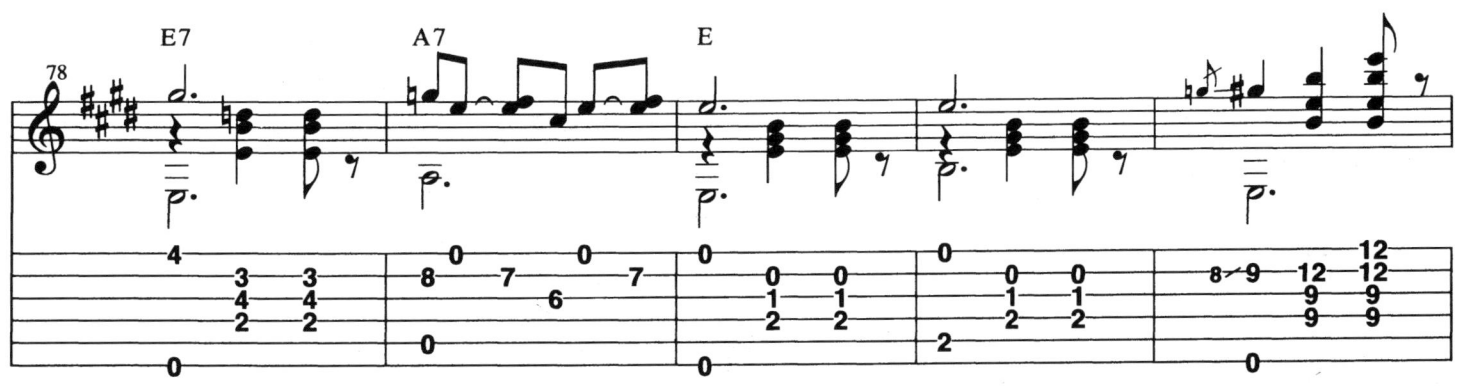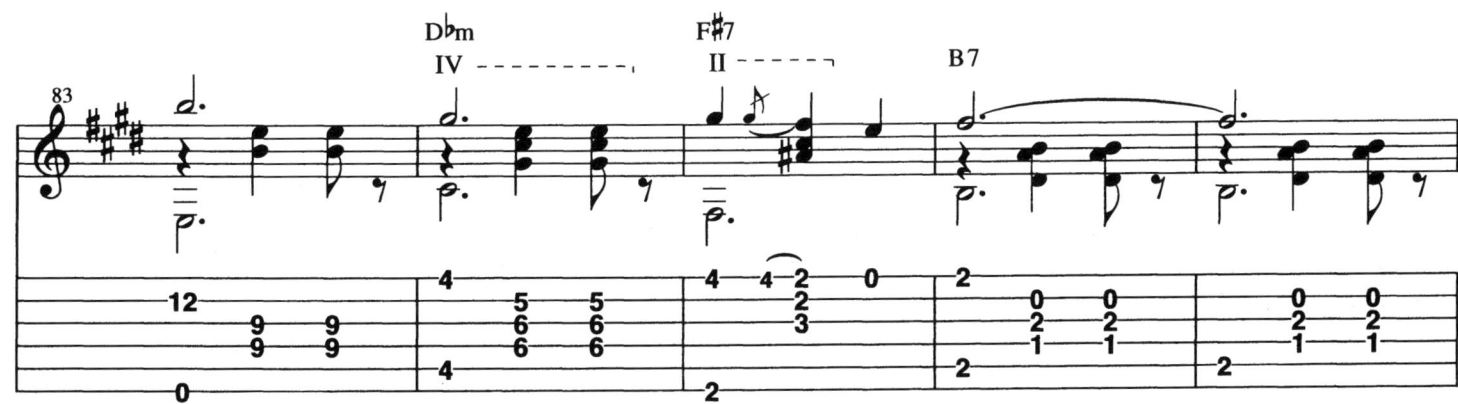

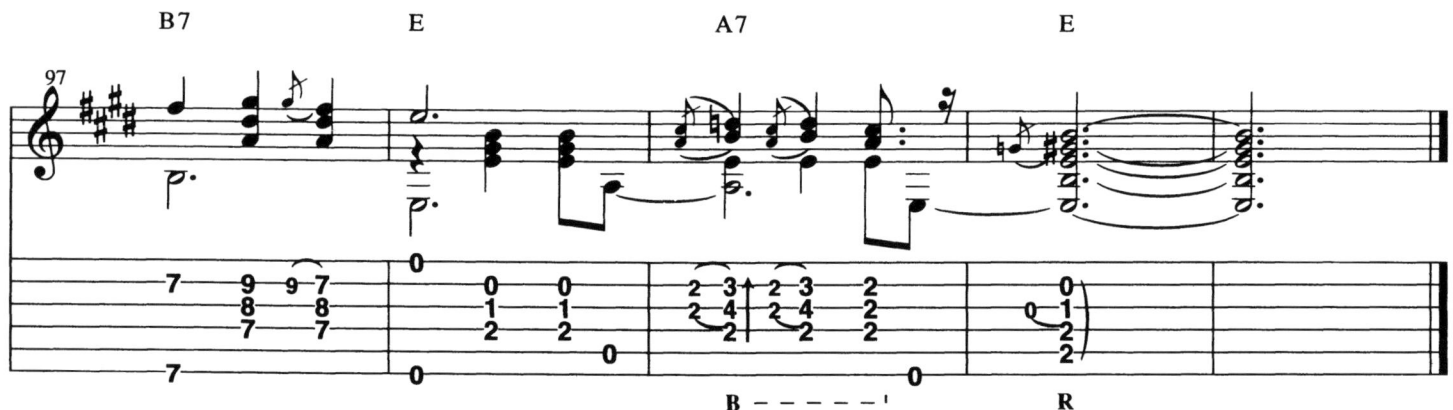

Performance Notes

Measures 50 through 73 are offered here to simulate the harmonica solo by Charlie McCoy in the recording and are not actually a part of the recording.

Just A Closer Walk With Thee

Traditional
Arr. Chet Atkins

31

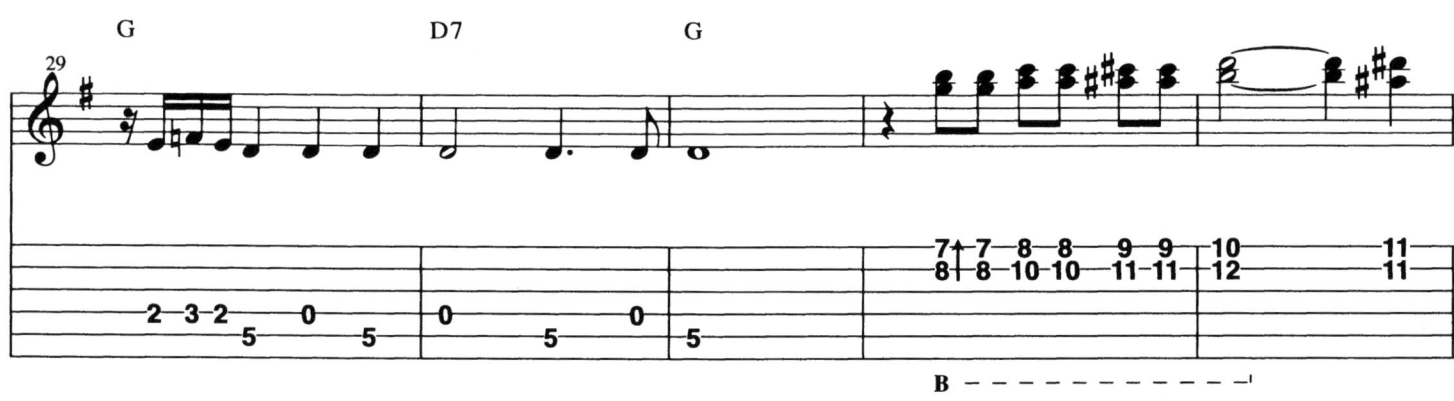
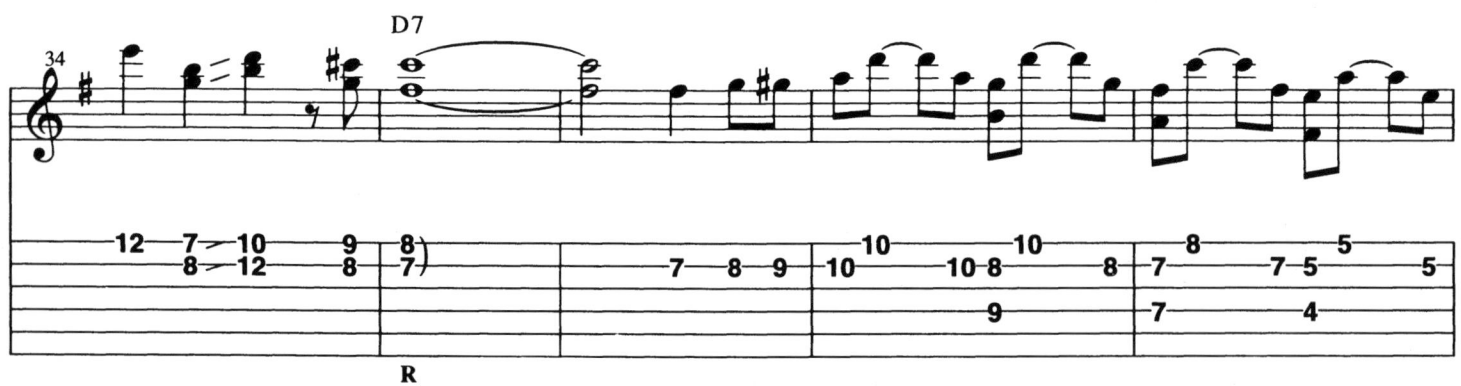

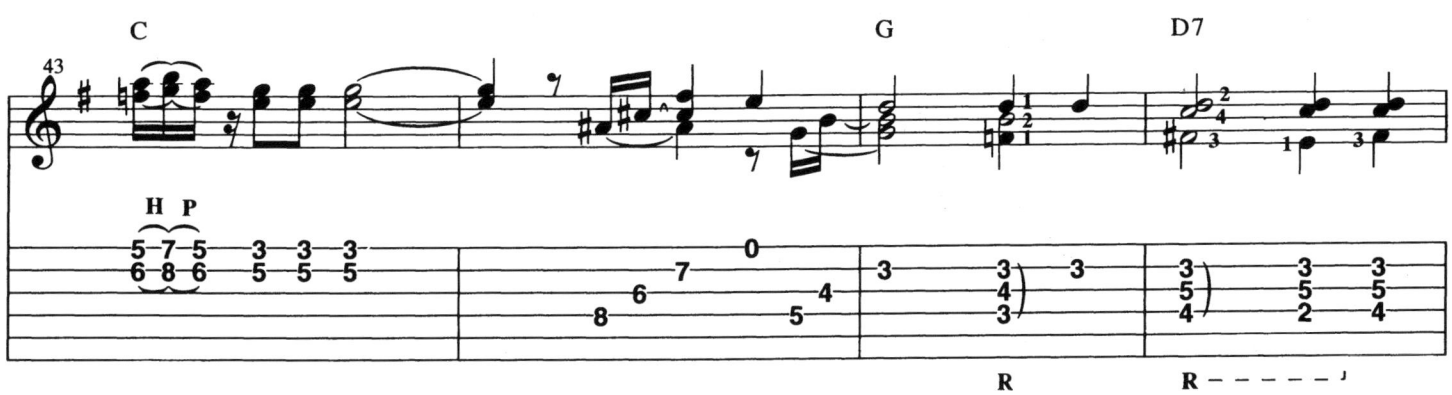

Performance Notes

The beautiful voicing in this arrangement requires several left hand stretches, so be prepared for a workout, especially in the opening measures of the piece. Pay attention to the left hand fingerings throughout as indicated by the numbers in the musical notation.

Photo by Don Corin

The Old Rugged Cross

Rev. George Bennard
Arr. Chet Atkins

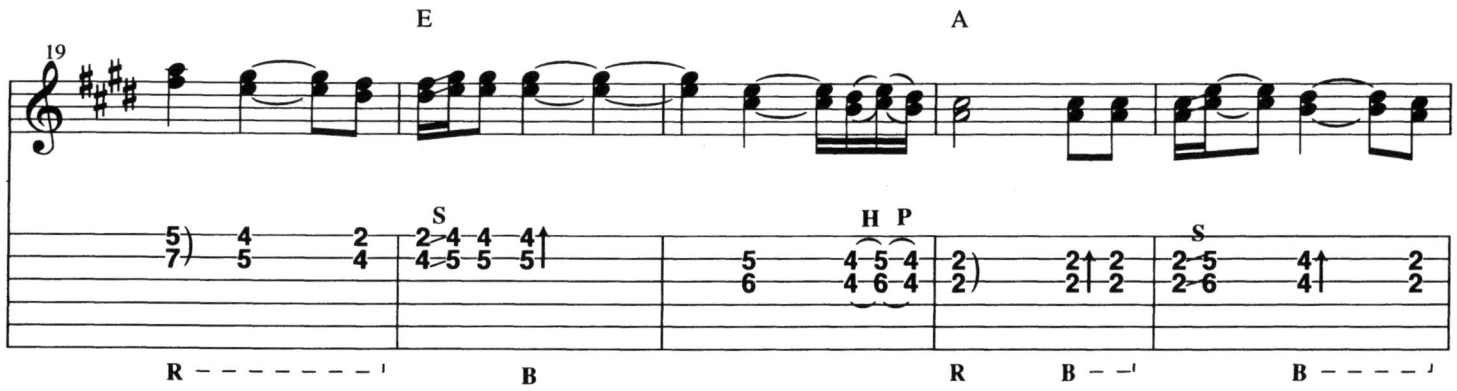

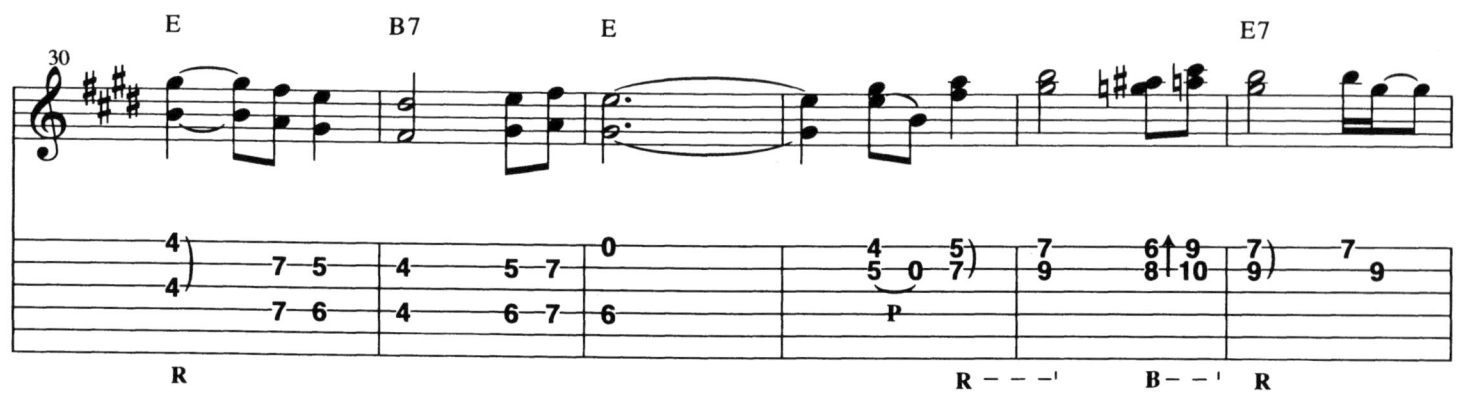
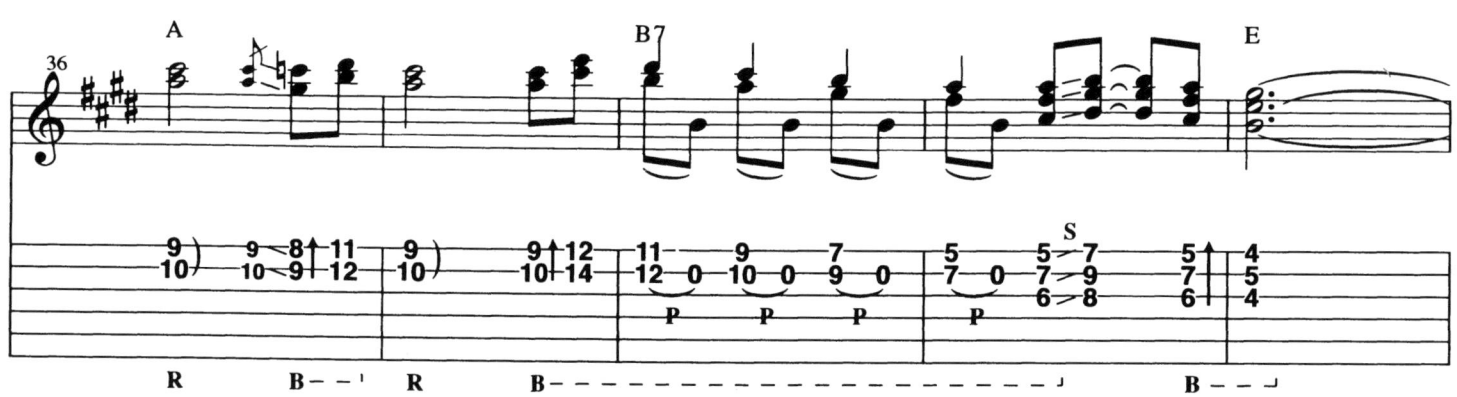

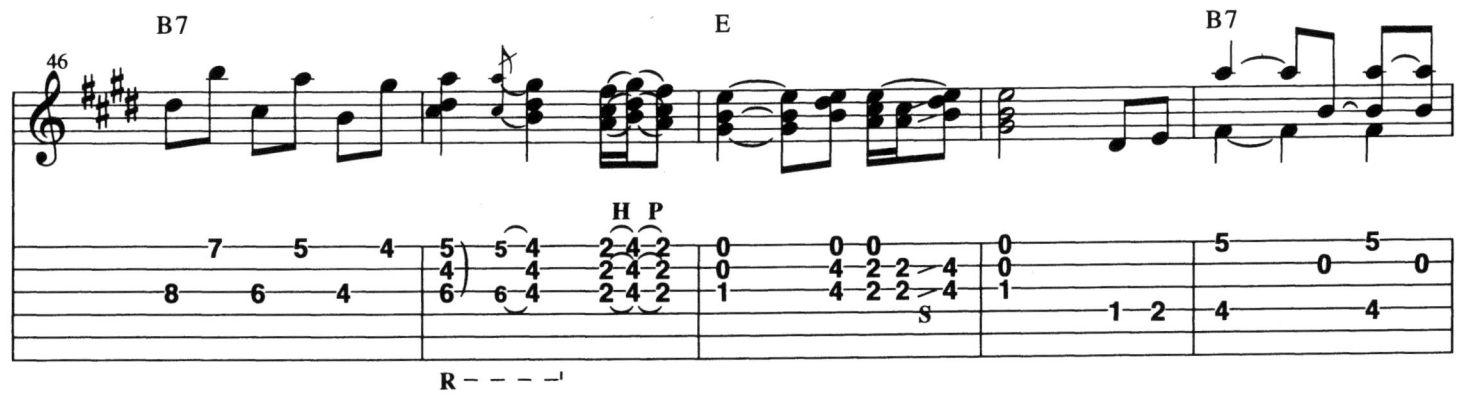
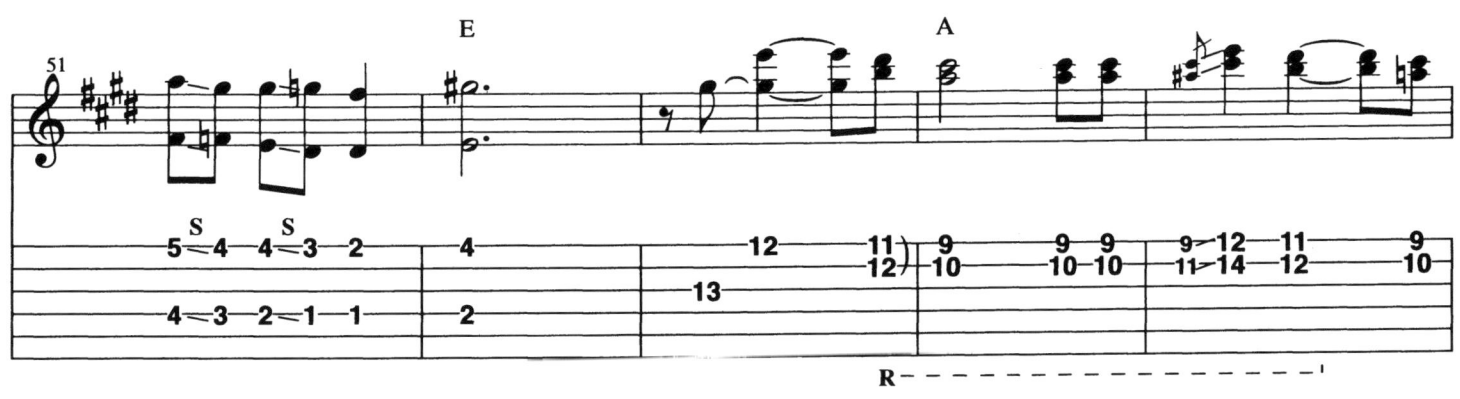

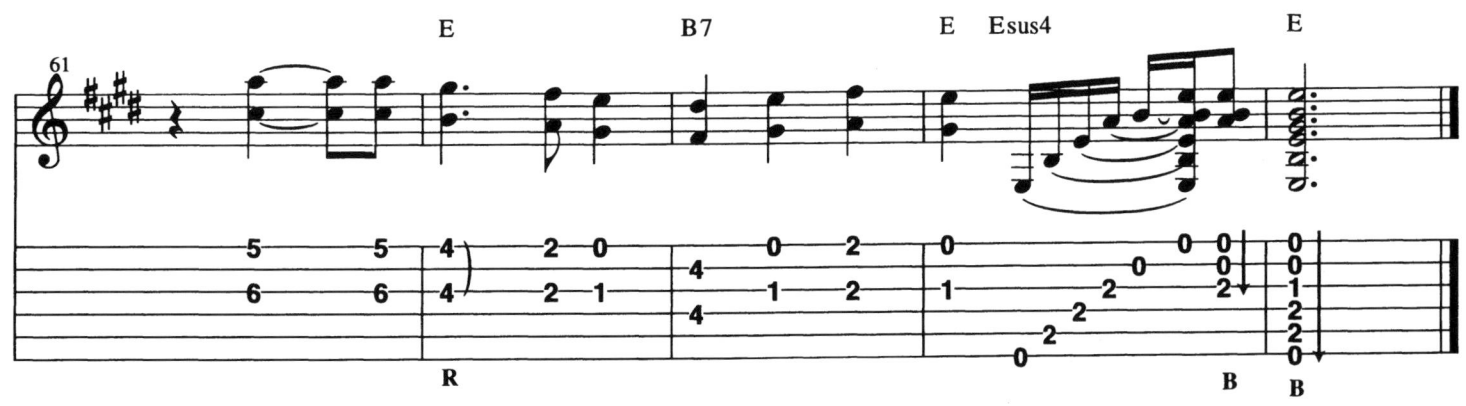

Lonesome Valley

Traditional

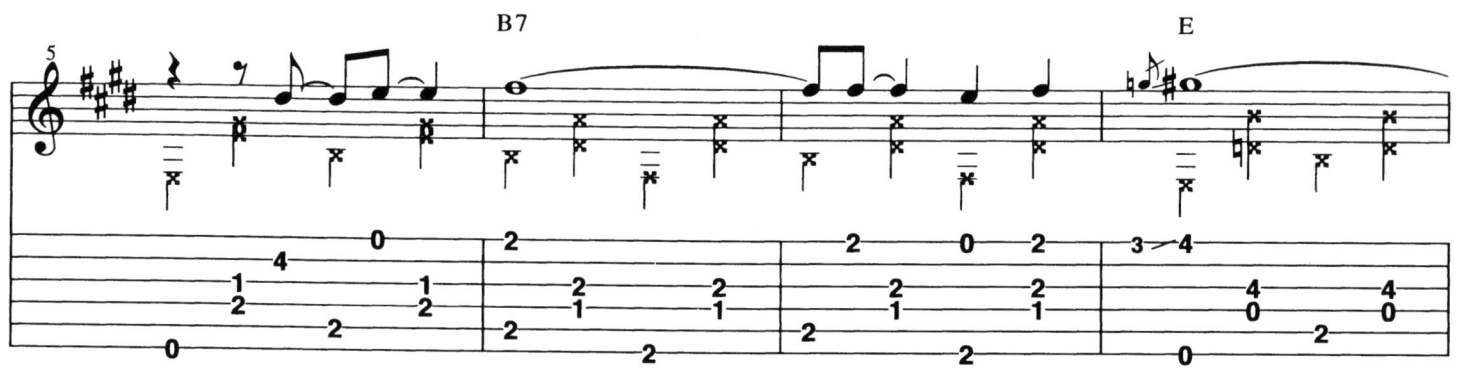
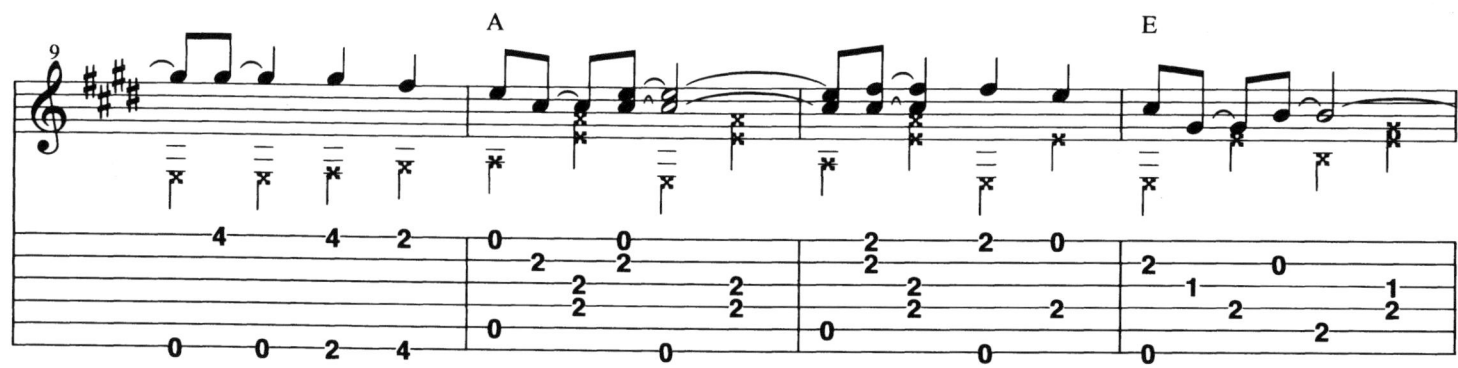
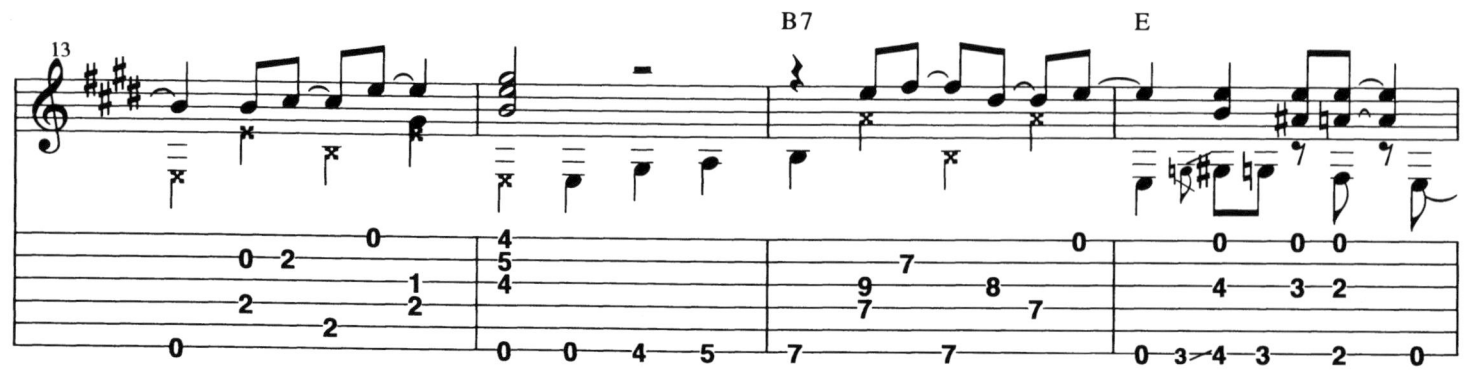

Arr. © 2001 by Athens Music Company. All Rights Reserved. Used by Permission.

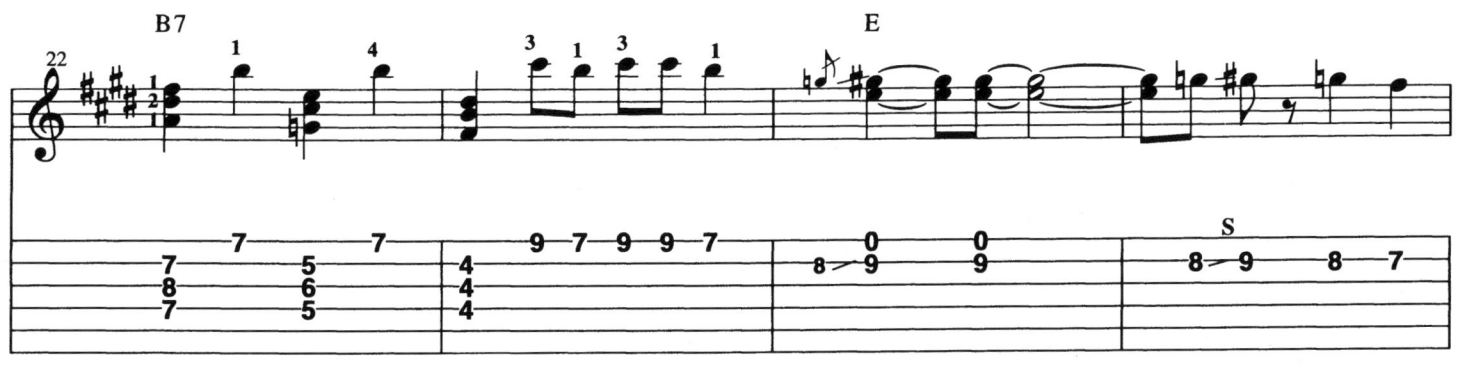

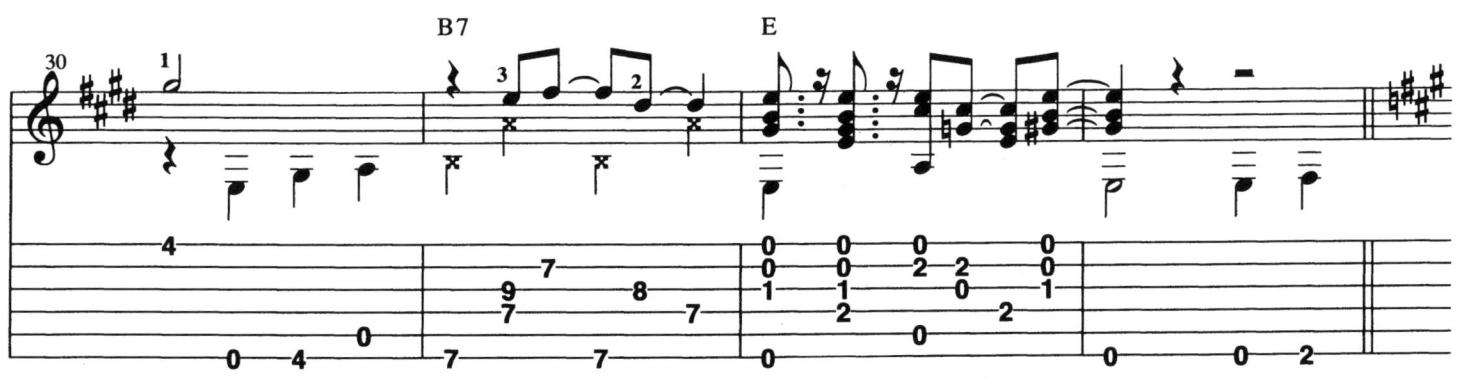

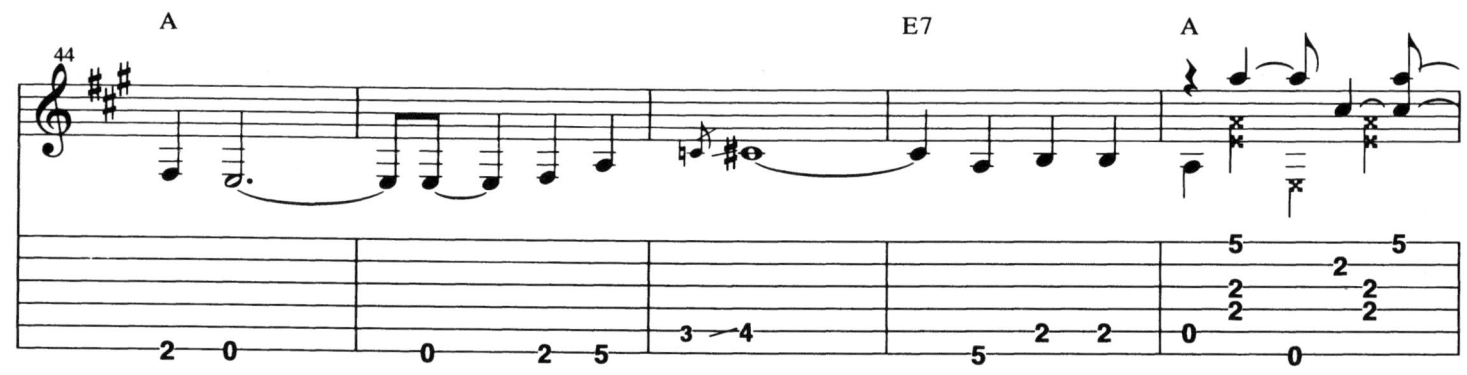
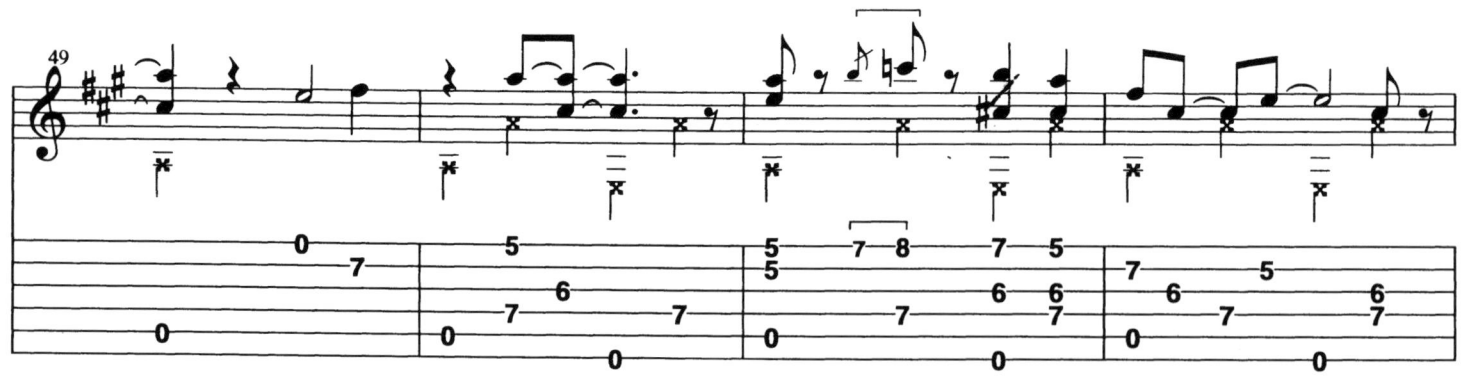

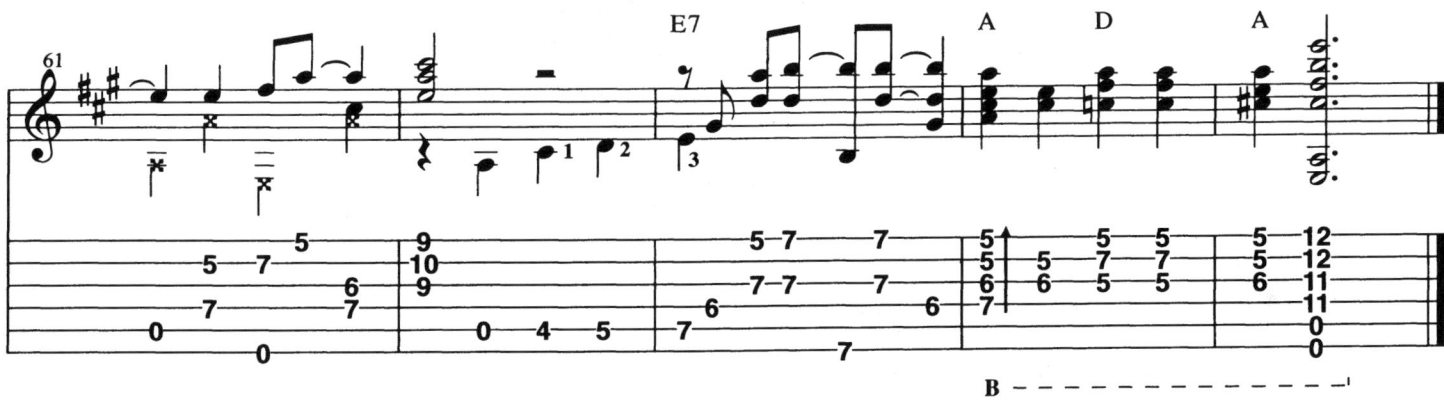

Performance Notes

This arrangement utilizes Chet's distinctive style of a steady rhythm alternating bass, which in 4/4 time is heard as "boom-chic, boom chic." Be sure to muffle the bass strings with the palm of the right hand. The melody line is played with the fingers against this steady bass rhythm. To avoid a mechanical feeling to the performance, listen to the recording carefully and note how Chet "anticipates the melody" to achieve a more easy going feel. Part of the secret is that the melody notes seldom fall directly on a beat. This may mean that the right hand fingers sound the strings just ahead of the thumb. After a little practice, the feeling should become spontaneous. These same techniques are used in the arrangement of *Will the Circle Be Unbroken*. The piece modulates to the key of A at measure 34. The measures of the recording that account for the harmonica solo are deleted from this transcription at measure 49.

Photo by Don Comp

God Be With You

Jeremiah Rankin
Arr. Chet Atkins

Arr. © 2001 by Athens Music Company. All Rights Reserved. Used by Permission.

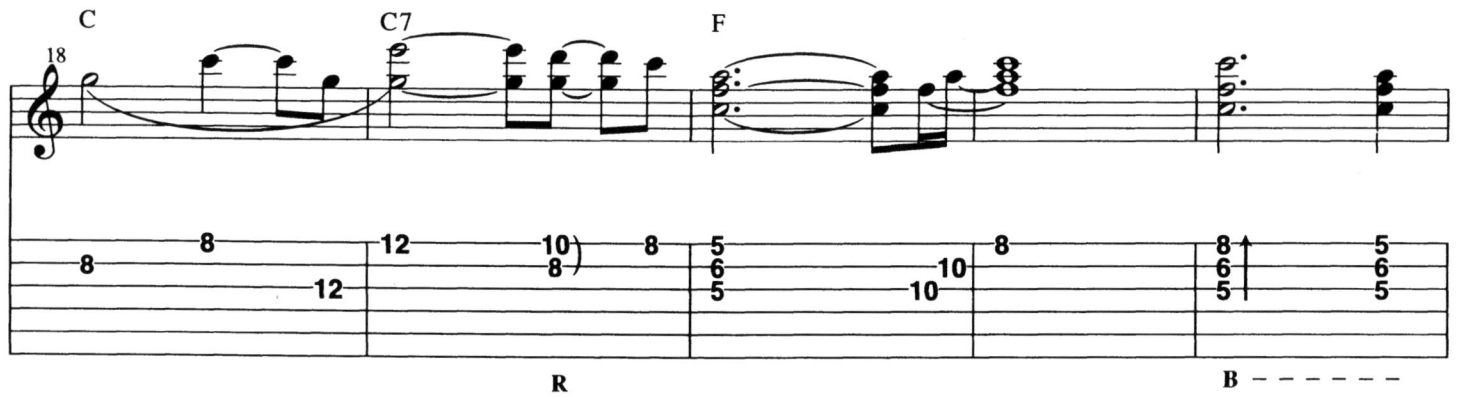
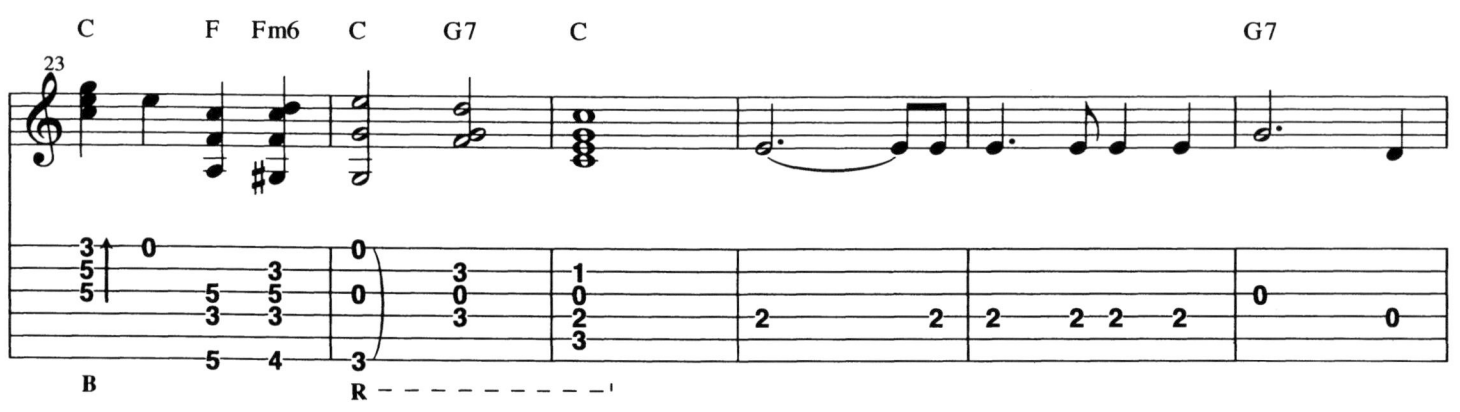

Performance Notes

This is probably the easiest arrangement on the album. It makes a terrific performance when combined with a rhythm guitar and bass after the opening lead guitar solo. The accompaniment chords are noted above the music staff.

Photo by Dan Comp

Were You There

Traditional
Arr. Chet Atkins

⑥ = D

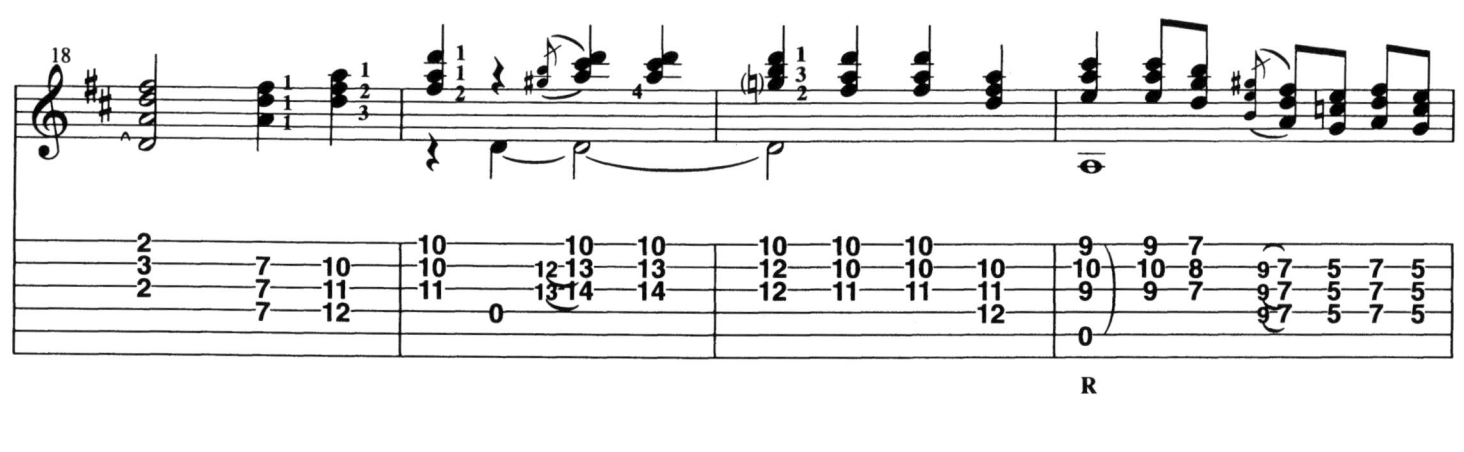
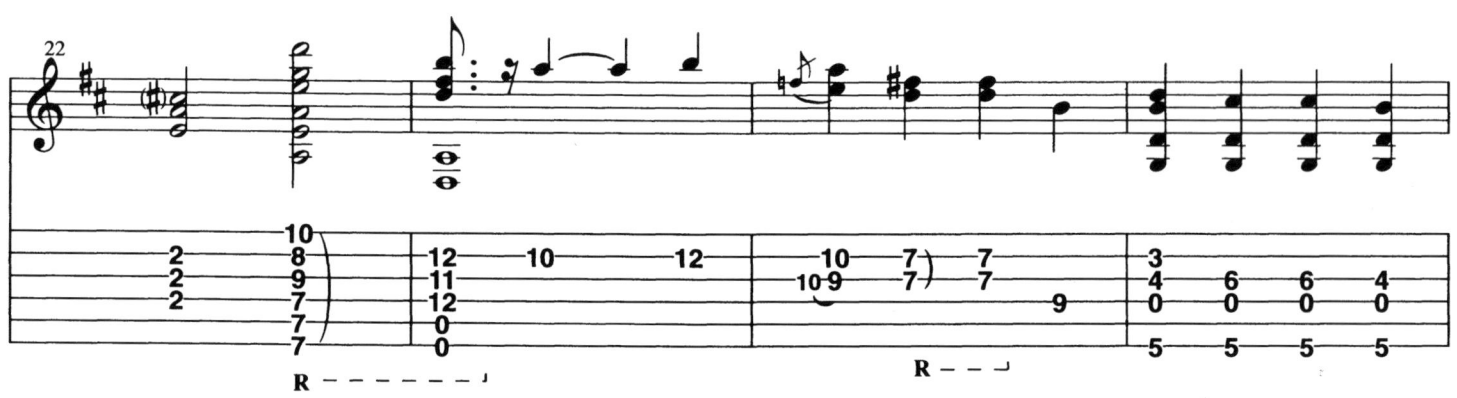
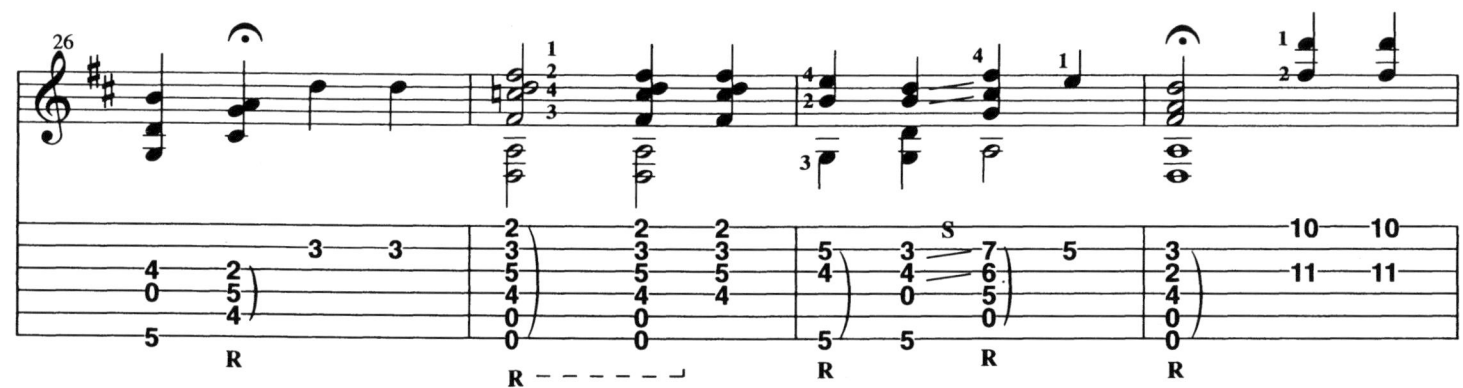
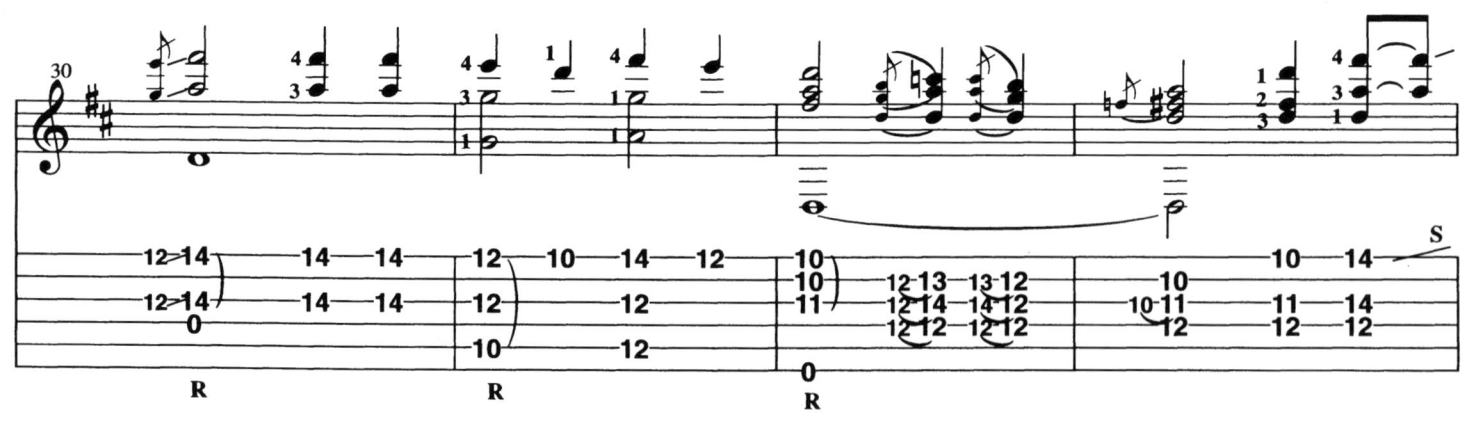

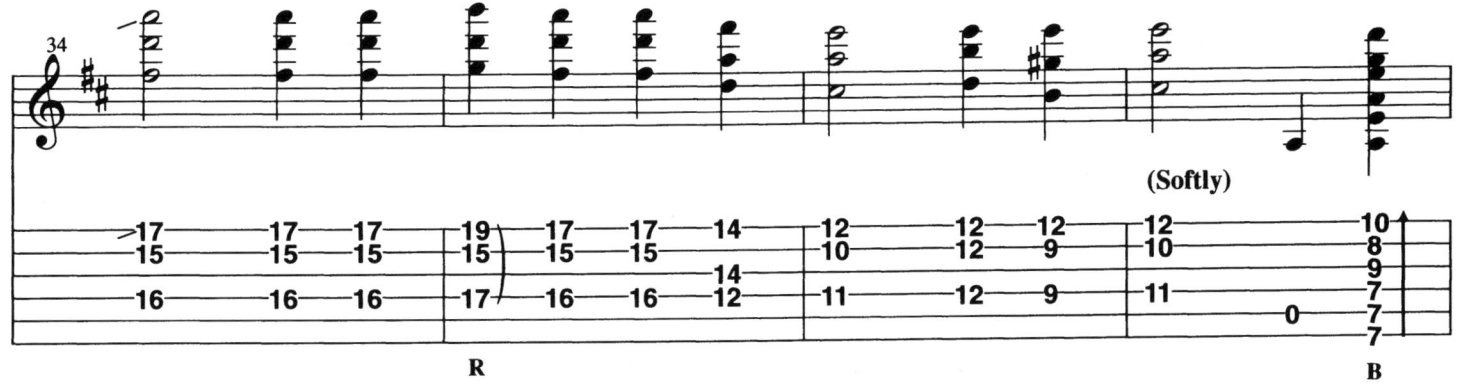

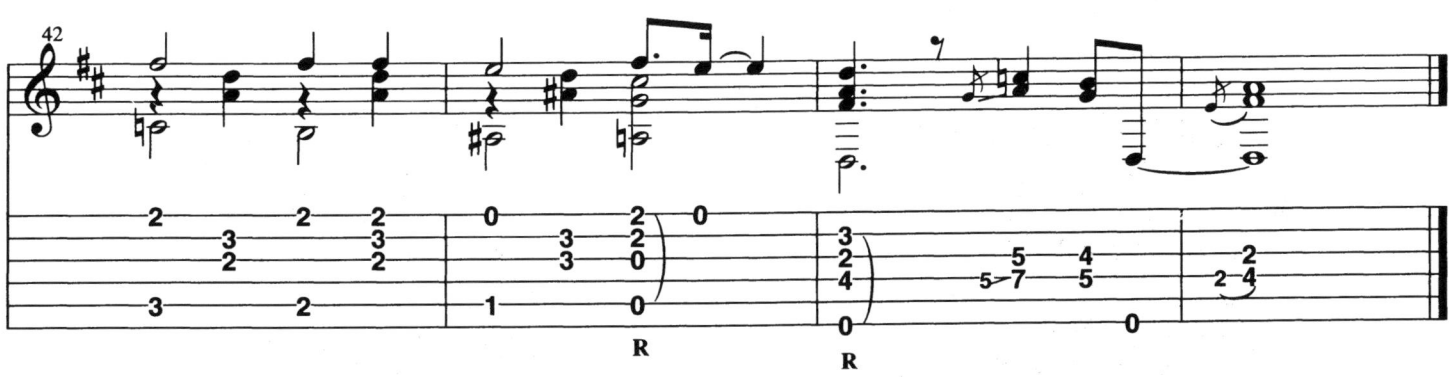

Performance Notes
Be sure to tune the sixth string to D. Left hand fingering is critical to this piece, especially measures 33-37. The numbers in the musical notation indicate the left hand fingering.

A Note From Craig Dobbins

"Chet Atkins Plays Back Home Hymns" features my favorite guitarist playing the music that's closest to my heart. For my friend, Jerry Ozee, putting these great Atkins arrangements to paper was a labor of love. He has played and honed these tunes for years, simply because he loves them. Now thanks to Jerry and the folks at Mel Bay, you can learn them too!

Thanks, Jerry, for transcribing these great hymns and gospel songs from a classic Atkins album!

Craig Dobbins

Craig Dobbins is the founder and publisher of Craig Dobbins' ACOUSTIC GUITAR WORKSHOP, P.O. Box 8075, Gadsden AL 35902. He is also the author of the book/CD set "Down Home Picking" MB96933BCD, "Fingerpicking Gospel Solos" MB98377BCD, and "The Jerry Reed Collection" MB98978.

Photo by Don Comp

A Note From Richard Hood

Buster Devault, Chet's best friend while growing up in Luttrell, Tennessee, told me about the times as a young boy when he would sit on his front porch on warm Saturday nights and hear music coming from the nearby Atkins' house that "sounded like the Grand Ole Opry." Lowell on guitar, Niona on piano, Chester on fiddle (and later on guitar), and the whole family would be singing. I can't help wondering if possibly just a few of those songs might have been hymns. I suspect they were... hymns like *Will the Circle Be Unbroken, In the Garden*, and *Amazing Grace*. It is no surprise then that Chet would eventually record an album of hymns and call it "Back Home..." Imagine that!

I can't tell you how many times I've listened to that album and wished that I could play those hymns like Chet. Now, thanks to Jerry Ozee's talent and commitment, at least I can play them. Play them like Chet? Not in a million years!

Dr. Richard Hood

Dr. Richard Hood presents a popular biographical multimedia presentation on the "Life and Times of Chet Atkins" at the annual Chet Atkins Appreciation Society Convention each summer in Nashville, TN.

Jerry Ozee, Richard Hood, and Bill Spann

My Favorite Chet Album

My favorite Chet Atkins album is *Chet Atkins Plays Back Home Hymns*. I have seen and heard this album touch people's souls like no other recording that I know of. I grew up in Houston, and spent many a Saturday afternoon from 1963-1967 at H&H Music Store, listening to local guitar legend Charlie Cash. I vowed then to learn this style if it took me 50 years! So before I left for Vietnam, I already had all of Chet's albums, except one. I didn't know then that I lacked one album, and therein lay an event that was to change my life.

After a tour of river patrol duty, I was in the Navy hospital in Sasebo, Japan, spiritually and mentally numb. One day I went to the little PX, looking for a Chet Atkins album to cheer me up. They had only one album, *Back Home Hymns*. I grew up in a church that used different hymns and no guitars. I put the vinyl on tape to take back with me for my 2nd tour, this time at Chau Doc, on the Cambodian border. We lived on a barge, and had a small stereo in our wardroom. My little tape immediately began to be played, mostly at night, mostly in headphones. Then, a miracle happened. A Navy chaplain gave me the words to the hymns. I'm so glad I didn't know the words already, because I might have repeated them more like a parrot than a lost soul. Mostly it was *In the Garden* that reached me. The tenderness and gentleness in these hymns soothed me as I learned for the first time that God "walks with me, talks with me, and tells me I am His own." Since Vietnam, I have been at countless men's retreats and seen tough guys weep when hearing this album for the first time. In our little wardroom at Chau Doc, I can remember many a young JG or Lieutenant, in a long dark night of the soul, listening in the dark to this album. Chet, you were there for us at Chau Doc, soothing and calming men who were tired, disillusioned and longing for peace.

What were the odds that one little PX in Sasebo, Japan, in May 1968, "just happened to have" that one album? What were the odds that this six-year-old vinyl album would minister so powerfully to a bunch of men who were seriously doubting their faith, ideals, guiding principles, and their hopes for a better world? To this day, no other resource touches my inner being like this beautiful album. It is out on CD now. Listen quietly to this album, and see how powerfully you are moved by Chet's gentle, loving touch.

Larry Oswald, Houston, TX

Reprinted with permission from *Mister Guitar*, the journal of the Chet Atkins Appreciation Society, February 2001.

About the Author

Jerry Ozee lives in Sullivan, Illinois, with his wife Shirley. He is a practicing dentist by profession, but his favorite pastime is the guitar, which he took up at age 11. Musically, he is mostly self-taught, but over the years he has gained the respect of many fine guitarists, and he has done some professional work himself. He has long admired the work of Chet Atkins, and among his favorite albums was the 1963 release of *Chet Atkins Plays Back Home Hymns* (RCA LPM/LSP-2601). Jerry has always tried to imitate Chet's perfection and has transcribed in this publication the entire selection of hymns note for note with *exacting* detail, just as they were recorded in the album. This labor of love is a tribute to the great Chet Atkins. The arrangements are beautiful and complete. By studying this work, one will gain new insight into the gifted genius of Chet Atkins, and will learn new skills at performing as well.

Jerry is a Charter Member of the Chet Atkins Appreciation Society, which meets each summer in Nashville, TN, and has consistently attended every convention over the years. At times he has performed for the group and has offered a workshop on playing some of Chet's tunes. For more information about the CAAS, write to The Chet Atkins Appreciation Society, c/o Mark Pritcher, 3716 Timberlake Road, Knoxville, TN 37920.

Photo by Don Camp

Discography

Chet Atkins Plays Back Home Hymns, RCA LPM/LSP 2601. Reissued on CD (BMG-1998 — 446802).

Some great sources for reissue CDs or the original vinyl LPs are:

Funky Junk Records, 698 Airline Road, McDonough GA 30253 (www.funkyjunk.com)

Guitar Records, PO Box 422, New Ellenton SC 29809 (www.guitarrecords.com)

General Gentry, 4588 Norris Freeway, Powell TN 37849

Buster DeVault, Jerry Ozee, and Chet Atkins
(Buster DeVault is Chet's life-long friend since boyhood in Luttrell, Tennessee)

Liner Notes from the Original LP
RCA LPM/LSP-2601

King Saul's servants had a wonderful suggestion for a way to relieve their king of evil spirits that troubled him. They said that he should "…seek out a man, who is a cunning player on an harp…" (I Samuel, 16:16) and he would, after listening to the music, feel much better. King Saul commanded them to go and find such a man.

One of the servants suggested a young shepherd he'd seen. His name was David and he lived in Bethlehem. The young man was finally brought to play for the king. "And it came to pass, when the evil spirit… was upon Saul, that David took an harp, and played with his hand: so Saul was refreshed, and was well, and the evil spirit departed from him." (I Samuel 16:23)

I have a good idea of how the mighty King Saul must have felt when he heard the inspired playing by the talented young David, for I have just listened to the twelve religious selections in this album played by Chet Atkins.

Every selection is superbly rendered, and not one is unfamiliar. To me, as to Chet, these melodies are a part of my heritage. I've heard them sung by quartets and choirs, played on pianos and organs. I've even heard my mother hum them as she went about her daily chores. But when Chet plays them they become a musical masterpiece in sacred sweetness.

I have known and idolized Chet for a good many years. Thousands of words of praise have been written about him. That's not nearly enough. Little David, the shepherd, became a king. So has Chet Atkins, the undisputed king of the guitar.

Merle Travis

Copyright RCA Records Nashville. Used by Permission.

Chet Atkins and Jerry Ozee

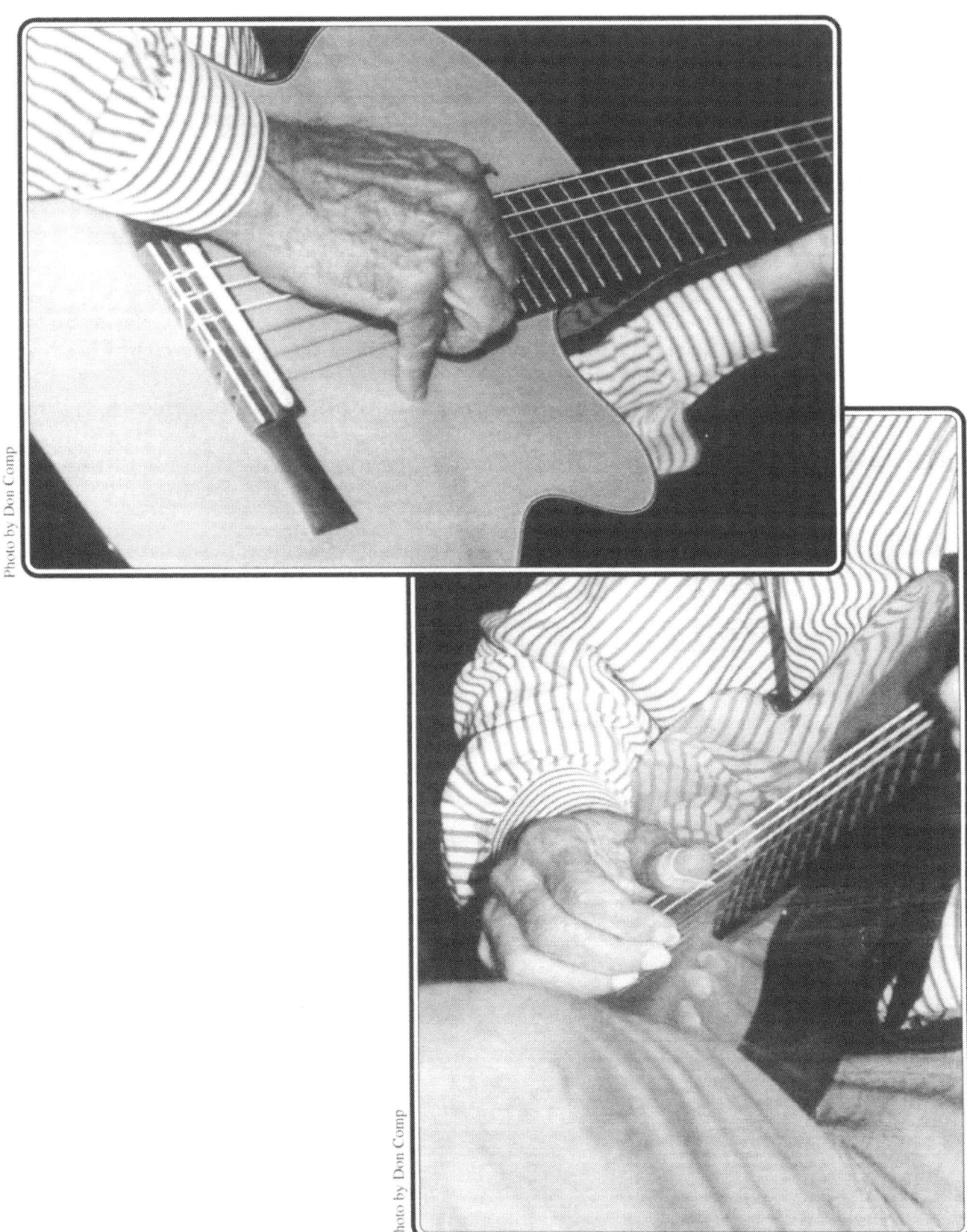